Response to Instructional Strategies and Interventions

Response to Instructional Strategies and Interventions

Scenarios for K–12 Educators

LINDA A. GREGG

with a contribution by
LYNN F. HOWARD

LEAD+
LEARN
PRESS

ENGLEWOOD, COLORADO

The Leadership and Learning Center
317 Inverness Way South, Suite 150
Englewood, Colorado 80112
Phone 1.866.399.6019 | Fax 303.504.9417
www.LeadandLearn.com

Published by Lead + Learn Press, a division of Houghton Mifflin Harcourt.

Library of Congress Cataloging-in-Publication Data

Gregg, Linda A.
  Response to instructional strategies and interventions : scenarios for K-12 educators / Linda A. Gregg ; with a contribution by Lynn F. Howard.
     p. cm.
  Includes bibliographical references and index.
  ISBN 978-1-933196-98-5 (alk. paper)
1. Response to intervention (Learning disabled children) 2. Special education.
3. Individualized instruction. I. Title.
  LC4705.G76 2012
  371.9—dc23

2012009419

ISBN 978-1-933196-98-5

Printed in the United States of America

16 15 14 13 12   01 02 03 04 05 06 07

Contents

Student Scenarios

PRIMARY (Pre-K–Grade 2)	UPPER ELEMENTARY (Grades 3–6)	SECONDARY (Grades 7–12)
CHAPTER ONE—TIER 1 SCENARIOS		
Writing	Note Taking	Spelling
CHAPTER TWO—TIER 2 SCENARIOS		
Number Sense	Mathematics	Mathematics
CHAPTER THREE—TIER 3 SCENARIOS		
Phonemic Awareness	Reading Comprehension	Writing
CHAPTER FOUR—SPECIAL EDUCATION SCENARIOS		
Sequencing Information	Mathematics	Reading
CHAPTER FIVE—GIFTED AND TALENTED SCENARIOS		
Mathematics	Writing	Mathematics
CHAPTER SIX—ENGLISH LANGUAGE LEARNER SCENARIOS		
Reading Fluency	Reading Comprehension	Reading

Foreword

Linda Gregg describes a practical down-to-earth perspective to address the national call for schools to focus on quality instruction for all students. She provides suggestions and tips that can be used in a variety of classroom settings. Response to Intervention may be seen as a complex system, but Linda manages to skillfully dispel myths and misconceptions and always keeps her eye firmly on the student.

The style of the book is friendly and provides numerous scenarios in which the reader will be able to identify with a variety of situations from elementary through high school. She frequently emphasizes the fact that "one size does not fit all" and demonstrates that point clearly in the multiple instructional strategies and interventions represented in each chapter.

Whether you are an elementary or secondary educator you will find the examples in each of the student scenarios instructive. The book provides "food for thought" and in some cases a confirmation of the practices you currently have in place. There may also be a point of clarification or a total shift in perspective from business as usual. She reminds us that we have a unique opportunity with Response to Intervention to have a tremendous impact on student achievement. Linda enthusiastically describes the conversation between teachers or parents and teachers and other school personnel all involved in providing the most appropriate intervention strategies for the students.

Throughout the book Linda uses students in multiple tiers, as well as English Language Learners (ELLs), special education students, and gifted students to provide strategies to help the reader understand how collaboration, assessment, selection of appropriate scientifically research-based strategies, delivery of instruction, and progress monitoring could take place in multiple settings.

Response to Instructional Strategies and Interventions: Scenarios for K–12 Educators provides a real-world method of unraveling the theoretical aspects of the 2004 reauthorization of the Individuals with Disabilities Act. It brings a clear focus on the adult actions that impact student performance. The reader will find the scenarios to be very engaging and informative. Linda Gregg deftly helps the reader see how the use of appropriately structured instruction and intervention strategies and effective collaboration allow students to learn.

—LYNN HOWARD

Preface

Response to Instructional Strategies and Interventions: Scenarios for K–12 Educators teaches practitioners how to effectively implement a multitier model of academic instruction for K–12 students. Response to Intervention (RTI) will be explained through the core principles of intervention described by the The National Center on RTI that include, but are not limited to, the following:

- High-quality, research-based classroom instruction
- Student assessment with classroom focus
- Universal screening of academics and behavior
- Continuous progress monitoring of students
- Implementation of appropriate research-based interventions
- Progress monitoring during interventions
- Teaching behavior fidelity

Response to Instructional Strategies and Interventions: Scenarios for K–12 Educators teaches practitioners how to effectively select intervention strategies aligned with current evidence of student learning. This book includes a process for selecting and implementing interventions for students in multiple tiers of academic performance. Intervention strategies are selected based on a collaborative process of inquiry and problem solving.

Readers will be provided with several opportunities to read about and follow the collaborative model, which includes collecting and analyzing data, setting appropriate goals, selecting instructional interventions, and monitoring student progress. This interactive book will provide ample opportunity for readers to understand the principles of RTI as well as practice with 18 multiage, multitiered scenarios. Following each scenario are research-based strategies that support each vignette. At the conclusion of this book, readers will be able to understand how to select appropriate instructional strategies and interventions and monitor the RTI process with skill and confidence.

Acknowledgments

Linda A. Gregg would like to sincerely thank Lynn Howard for her support and contributions to this project. She would also like to recognize and sincerely thank the following individuals who contributed to the content and publication of this work: Larry Ainsworth, Lisa Almeida, Kristin Anderson, Laura Besser, Lauren Campsen, Brandon Doubek, Cheryl Dunkle, Lillian Hawkins, Wallace Howard, Connie Kamm, Debbie Lee, Peggy Lush, Herb Miller, Liz Monsma, Mary Jane O'Connell, Linda O'Konek, Angela Peery, Thommie Piercy, Douglas Reeves, Kelly Valentine, Mary Vedra, Joan Anderson, Joseph McGuill, and Katie Stoddard.

Tremendous appreciation to the Response to Instructional Strategies and Intervention Focus Group—Sheri, Callan, Katie, Beth, Patty, Dee, Nikki, and Diana of the Englewood School District in Englewood, Colorado—for their time, knowledge, skill, and enthusiastic dedication to this project.

Special thanks and deep appreciation to the publication team of Lead + Learn Press.

About the Authors

Linda A. Gregg is a Senior Professional Development Associate with The Leadership and Learning Center. She is also the Director of Education for Villa Santa Maria, a residential treatment center in New Mexico. She is the author of "Crossing the Canyon: Helping Students with Special Needs Achieve," a chapter in *Ahead of the Curve: The Power of Assessment to Transform Teacher and Learning.* Linda is also the author of "RTI Meets Data Teams," a chapter in *Data Teams: The Big Picture,* and the "Power Strategies for Response to Intervention" seminar.

Linda holds professional credentials in general education, special education, and school administration. She has taught elementary through high school and has served as an elementary and high school principal. She is a former Associate Superintendent of Federal Programs and Assistant Professor and Coordinator of the Special Education Program at the College of Santa Fe in New Mexico.

As a Professional Development Associate, Linda is recognized for her expertise in working with diverse learners and bridging the achievement gap for students in special education. She is a regional, national, and international speaker as well as a Leadership Performance Coach. Linda has conducted numerous interactive, hands-on workshops, including "Data Teams," "Decision Making for Results," "Power Strategies for Effective Teaching," "'Unwrapping' the Standards," "Engaging Classroom Assessments," "Common Formative Assessments," "Effective Grading Practices," "Making Differentiated Instruction Work," and "Effective Implementation of Response to Intervention."

Lynn F. Howard is a Professional Development Associate with The Leadership and Learning Center. She worked in the Charlotte–Mecklenburg School System for more than 30 years as a middle grades science teacher, coordinator of the gifted program, and a regional assistant superintendent for middle schools. Lynn has conducted extensive staff development programs around the country and has brought a wealth of experience to schools and districts including improving planning and teaming, leadership and relationship building, and systemic school-reform strategies. As a presenter for the National Speakers Bureau for Geoscience

Education, Lynn has provided seminars and workshops on best instructional practices and effective site-based teacher-retention programs. And as someone who has survived being locked in an outhouse miles from civilization, she brings an adventurous approach to the real-life strategies for teaching and learning.

Lynn holds a Master's Degree in Earth Science and Education and a Bachelor's Degree in Biology from the University of North Carolina at Charlotte, Academy Certification from the National Staff Development Council, and National Certification in Gifted and Talented.

Ready for Anything: Supporting New Teachers for Success is Lynn's first book, and she has also authored the three-book series, *Five Easy Steps to a Balanced Science Program*. With a passion for helping first-year teachers, Lynn is an advocate for those entering the teaching profession.

Introduction

Response to Instructional Strategies and Interventions: Scenarios for K–12 Educators addresses two Essential Questions:

► How does Response to Intervention (RTI) affect teaching and learning for all students?

► How can the principles of RTI be immediately implemented in the classroom?

Response to Intervention is a framework that guides instruction for *all* students. It is the practice of providing high-quality instruction and interventions matched to student needs. RTI is also the practice of frequently monitoring progress to make decisions about the need for possible changes in instruction or goals and applying student response data to make important educational decisions. RTI should be applied to decisions in general education, remedial education, and special education. The goal is to create a well-integrated system of instruction and intervention guided by data on student outcome (National Association of State Directors of Special Education [NASDSE], 2006).

Response to Intervention is a multitiered approach to providing services and interventions at increasing levels of intensity to students who require supplemental learning. The progress that each student makes at each stage of intervention should be closely monitored. Results of this monitoring are used to make decisions about the need for further research-based instruction and/or intervention in general education, special education, or both.

The RTI process is depicted graphically in several ways throughout the United States. Typically, RTI is represented by a triangle or pyramid shape. (See Exhibit I.1.) Sometimes, the base of the triangle or pyramid represents the Tier 1 universal students, with Tier 2 targeted students in the middle, and Tier 3 shown on top representing the level for intensive intervention. In some cases, however, you will see this same triangle with the image inverted. Either way, the expectation is that the vast majority (80 to 90 percent) of students (Tier 1) will be able to respond to the highly qualified general education teacher's scientifically research-based instructional strategies and interventions.

This resource can be used for individual learning, book study, or workshop sessions. There are 18 scenarios describing students in K–12 grade levels. Each

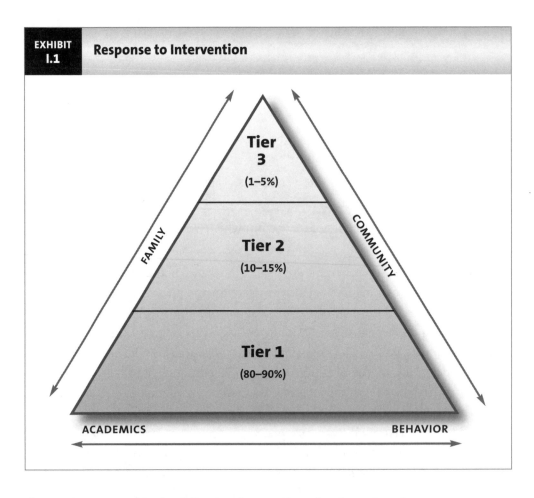

EXHIBIT I.1 — **Response to Intervention**

(Pyramid diagram: Tier 3 (1–5%) at top, Tier 2 (10–15%) in middle, Tier 1 (80–90%) at bottom. Left side labeled FAMILY, right side labeled COMMUNITY, base labeled ACADEMICS on the left and BEHAVIOR on the right.)

chapter is presented in the following format: Introduction of a primary, upper elementary, and secondary student; brief discussion of the student issues related through the concerns of the classroom teacher; and a description of the grade-level or content department team meeting. Next the reader will see a chart of research- or evidence-based instructional strategies and interventions discussed by the student's teacher and grade-level or content team members. Immediately following the list of sample strategies is a discussion of how the selected strategy was implemented (**Implementation Tip**) by the student's teacher under the heading **"How does it look?"** This details the steps that the educator took to use the strategy in the classroom. Next, under the heading **"How is it monitored?"** is a description of how the strategy was progress monitored. Following each section readers will find the **"How have you thought about?"** section where guiding questions allow readers to connect the scenarios to their own settings. Throughout the book there are references to graphic organizers or forms that may be immediately referenced for your convenience in the appendices.

Chapter 1 describes a variety of instructional strategies that the general education teacher might use to address the needs of diverse learners in Tier 1. Scenarios include writing strategies for pre-K–grade 2, note taking for grades 3–6, and spelling in grades 7–12.

Chapter 2 explains how to select and use Tier 2 (targeted) intervention strategies for those students who did not respond as expected to the core Tier 1 instruction. There are three scenarios in Chapter 2 that provide examples of pre-K–grade 2 number sense, grades 3–6 mathematics, and grades 7–12 mathematics.

Chapter 3 addresses the needs of students who have not responded with proficiency to core Tier 1 differentiated instruction or the targeted intervention strategies of Tier 2. Scenarios in this chapter for Tier 3 include intensive intervention strategies for pre-K–grade 2 phonemic awareness, grades 3–6 reading comprehension, and grades 7–12 writing.

Chapter 4 depicts a range of students eligible for special education services. Scenarios include Tier 1 instructional strategies for pre-K–grade 2 students learning to sequence information. It also describes targeted Tier 2 instructional interventions in mathematics for students in grades 3–6, and intensive Tier 3 reading intervention strategies for grades 7–12 students.

Chapter 5 discusses students who are eligible for services as Gifted and Talented with a variety of instructional needs. Their individual needs may be met through differentiated Tier 1 instruction, Tier 2 targeted intervention strategies, or Tier 3 intensive intervention strategies. The intervention is supplemental support for students not reaching their expected potential, or it may be enrichment for those who have exceeded their classmates. Scenarios in this chapter include pre-K–grade 2 mathematics, grades 3–6 writing, and grades 7–12 mathematics.

Chapter 6 focuses on intervention strategies for K–12 English Language Learners, including pre-K–grade 2 reading fluency, grades 3–6 reading comprehension, and grades 7–12 reading.

The grade-level or content department team meetings are briefly discussed in each chapter in an effort to allow the reader to see how the intervention strategies were selected by the team. The grade-level or content department team is a collaboration of two or more professionals who share their expertise in order to implement instructional or behavioral strategies to benefit student learning. Teams follow a process for their meetings:

1. Collect and conduct ongoing assessment of data.
   (See Appendix D, Sample Universal Screening Instruments.)

2. Analyze assessed strengths and challenges to determine root causes.

a. What have you observed?

b. What information does the data provide?

c. What are the strengths, challenges, and inferences?

d. What is the root cause?

During this step of analysis, the team should look for dependent and independent variables. Identifying independent and dependent variables will guide the team in determining which elements may be influenced or modified by intervention.

3. Establish SMART (Specific, Measureable, Achievable, Relevant and Timely) goals. Set, review, and revise goals.

4. Select scientifically research-based instructional strategies and interventions.

5. Progress monitor planned before, during, and after intervention.

My goal in presenting Response to Intervention (I refer to it as Response to Instructional Strategies and Intervention) is as a series of scenarios to provide the reader with the opportunity to experience a range of depictions of how RTI is addressed in K–12 classrooms. The book provides reflection questions that may be generalized to a variety of situations. Although these scenarios provide an abbreviated list of intervention strategies, there are additional resources in the appendices that may address the individual needs of your students.

As a companion to the book, a comprehensive Response to Instructional Strategies and Intervention seminar is offered through The Leadership and Learning Center. This seminar includes specific research-based strategies, intervention and progress monitoring tools, and real-world video clips of students and teachers practicing RTI.

Overview

Response to Intervention offers school districts the benefits of providing screening, interventions, and varied service-delivery models to all students based on their individual needs. Most students (80 to 90 percent) respond successfully to interventions that have been scientifically validated, but how should a teacher intervene for the 10 to 20 percent of students who need a more targeted intervention to succeed? How should the teacher identify those students who require more intensive interventions in the general education classroom?

With the reauthorization of the federal Individuals with Disabilities Education Improvement Act (IDEIA), signed into law in December 2004, came changes to the process of identifying students with specific learning disabilities (SLD). Previously, students in most districts were identified with a discrepancy model. A discrepancy model is described as a severe discrepancy between achievement and intellectual ability. Response to instructional interventions has eliminated the "wait to fail" issue by requesting that teachers provide early intervention. Each state has determined how it will address the discrepancy model. www.rti4success.org offers a database that shows which model is used by each state. Based on the reauthorization, states may continue to use the standard discrepancy model, or they may also use (or use instead) research-based interventions eligibility for services for a specific learning disability.

Because of the new option permitted by the reauthorization for determining student eligibility for services for SLD, the exclusive reliance on assessment has been supplemented by the use of scientifically research-based instruction conducted by a highly qualified general-education teacher. Response to Intervention is a concept similar to many concepts in medical models in which teams focus on the patient's response to treatment.

At first glance, one might think that RTI is a special education initiative, but the language in the reauthorization of the IDEIA made it clear that early intervention should occur initially within the general-education classroom rather than being limited to the environment. Early intervention is not limited to extreme cases nor is it limited to preschool programs or primary school students.

According to IDEIA, 614, b, 6, A, B 2 (IDEIA, 2004):

(A) When determining whether a child has a specific learning disability as defined in section 602, a local education agency (LEA) shall not be required to take into consideration whether a child has a severe discrepancy between achievement and intellectual ability in oral expression, listening comprehension, written expression, basic reading skill, reading comprehension, mathematical calculation, or mathematical reasoning.

(B) Additionally, in determining whether a child has a specific learning disability, a local educational agency (or school district) may use a process that determines whether the child responds to scientific, research-based interventions as a part of the evaluation procedures.

The IDEIA's definition of *specific learning disabilities* indicates that prior to consideration for eligibility, it must be demonstrated that "the child was provided appropriate instruction in regular education settings" (IDEIA, 2004). Typically, this requirement is met by providing standards-based instruction by the general-education teacher to all students and then targeting or intensifying the level of instruction or intervention based on individual or small-group needs.

Response to Intervention: Key Elements and Definition

The key components of Response to Intervention suggested by the federal government include, but are not limited to:

► Universal screening of academics and behavior

► High-quality research-based classroom instruction

► Implementation of appropriate research-based interventions

► Student assessment with a classroom focus

► Continuous progress monitoring during interventions

► Teaching with fidelity

Definition

Response to Intervention (RTI) is a framework that guides instruction for *all* students. There are multiple definitions of RTI, including the following:

Response to Intervention is the practice of providing high-quality instruction and interventions matched to student need, monitoring progress frequently to make decisions about changes in instruction or goals, and applying student response data to important educational decisions.

The RTI process is a multistep approach to providing services and interventions at increasing levels of intensity to students who struggle with learning. Student progress, at each stage of intervention, is closely monitored. Results of this monitoring are used to make decisions about the need for further research-based instruction and/or intervention in general education.

The RTI process has the potential to limit the amount of academic failure that any student experiences and to increase the accuracy of evaluations. The use of RTI could also reduce the number of children who are mistakenly identified as having learning disabilities when their learning problems are due to cultural differences or lack of adequate instruction (National Center for Learning Disabilities [NCLD], 2006).

Description

IDEIA: Individuals with Disabilities Education Improvement Act of 2004 (also referred to as IDEA)

What is now known as the Individuals with Disabilities Education Improvement Act of 2004 (IDEIA) was originally passed in 1975 (and reauthorized in 2004). It is a federal statute relative to public education and services to students with disabilities, ages 3 through 21.

AYP: Adequate Yearly Progress

A statewide accountability system mandated by the No Child Left Behind Act of 2001 required each state to ensure that all schools and districts make adequate yearly progress (AYP), as defined by states and approved by the U.S. Department of Education. School districts are looking for a way to make sure that their students are making adequate yearly progress.

Overidentification

The term *overidentification* refers to the overrepresentation of students, above state and national averages, in programs and in services. This term indicates that the school or school district in question has identified a higher proportion of students for services through special education than the proportion of that population in the general population. The term *overidentification* also refers to the overrepresentation of students in specific disability-related categories, that is, at rates that are above state and national averages. Using a positive Response to Intervention model can help school districts proactively monitor the responses of students to general-education intervention strategies prior to referral for services.

Specific Learning Disability (SLD)

The child who does not achieve adequately for his or her age or does not meet state approved grade-level standards in one or more of the following areas is assessed as having a specific learning disability (SLD). This assessment is made only when the child has been provided with learning experiences and instruction appropriate age or based on state-approved grade-level standards in (i) oral expression, (ii) listening comprehension, (iii) written expression, (iv) basic reading skill, (v) reading fluency skills, (vi) reading comprehension, (vii) mathematics calculation, and (viii) mathematics problem solving (Specific Learning Disability, 2006).

Early Intervening Services (EIS)

The concept of early intervening services (EIS) was introduced in IDEIA 2004. EIS refers to a broad application of scientifically based prevention and support services for students who have not been identified as needing special education programs or services but who need additional academic and behavioral support to succeed in the general-education classroom.

No Child Left Behind (NCLB) states that "a local education agency (LEA) will provide training to enable teachers to teach and address the needs of students with different learning styles, particularly students with disabilities, students with special learning needs (including students who are gifted and talented), and students with limited English proficiency; and to improve student behavior in the classroom and identify early and appropriate interventions to help these students."

A local education agency may use up to 15 percent of its IDEIA Part B funds in any fiscal year, less any funds reduced from its local fiscal effort, to develop and implement coordinated early intervening services. Coordinated early intervening services may include interagency financing structures for students in K–12, with a particular emphasis on students in K–3, who have not been identified as needing special education or related services but who need additional academic and behavioral support to succeed in a general-education environment.

In cases in which a disproportionately large number of students have been identified as disabled or placed in special programs for the disabled, the state education agency (SEA) is required to intervene. In such cases, the SEA shall require the LEA to reserve the maximum 15 percent of IDEIA Part B funds to provide comprehensive, coordinated early intervening services to serve children in the LEA, particularly children in those groups that have been significantly overidentified.

EIS activities could include professional development for teachers and other school staff to deliver scientifically based academic instruction and behavioral interventions, including scientifically based literacy instruction.

ESEA/NCLB: Elementary and Secondary Education Act/No Child Left Behind

The Elementary and Secondary Education Act (ESEA), which was originally passed in 1965, was reauthorized in 2001 and renamed the No Child Left Behind (NCLB) Act of 2001.

The definition of Specific Learning Disabilities is as follows:

(10) *Specific learning disability*

(i) *General.* Specific learning disability means a disorder in one or more of the basic psychological processes involved in understanding or in using language, spoken or written, that may manifest itself in the imperfect ability to listen, think, speak, read, write, spell, or to do mathematical calculations, including conditions such as perceptual disabilities, brain injury, minimal brain dysfunction, dyslexia, and developmental aphasia.

(ii) *Disorders not included.* Specific learning disability does not include learning problems that are primarily the result of visual, hearing, or motor disabilities, of mental retardation, of emotional disturbance, or of environmental, cultural, or economic disadvantage (Specific Learning Disabilities/IDEIA, 2004).

UNIVERSAL SCREENING

The implementation of Response to Intervention (RTI) typically begins with the universal screening of all students to determine academic and/or behavioral progress. The purpose of this screening is to determine which students need academic or behavioral assistance. Although RTI includes both academic and behavioral issues, this book is dedicated to academic concerns. The universal screening provides the foundation for a variety of instructional decisions. Universal screenings should be administered three times a year, typically fall, winter, and spring. Universal screening is an assessment made by administering quick, low-cost, repeatable tests of age-appropriate critical skills or behaviors to all students. Measures are not too complicated and can be administered by someone with a minimal amount of training.

The testing is administered to determine the effectiveness of curriculum, instruction, and school organization and to determine students' levels of proficiency in essential academic areas. Screening data are organized in a format that allows for the inspection of both group performance and individual student performance on specific skills.

Providing universal screening at the beginning of the school year, along with an appropriate system of rigorous intervention and progress monitoring, will ensure that the needs of all students are being met so that students are not overlooked due to lack of sufficient intervention.

Many schools have already established grade-level team meetings, Data Teams, or Professional Learning Communities (PLCs) to begin addressing the individual needs of students.

► The process shows how functional the core curriculum and instruction are in the school. In a multitiered model of school support, about 80 percent of all students in the school should be showing adequate progress while using a particular curricular element or program. If more than 20 percent of the students are not making acceptable gains in an area, the school must improve its core curriculum and/or the manner in which the curriculum is delivered to the students.

► Second, universal screening identifies those students who are not making acceptable progress in the core curriculum. Provided that 80 percent or more are making adequate progress in the foundational curriculum, those who are not require additional intervention, either in small groups or on an individual basis.

Universal screens may be repeated with a small group of students to determine whether lower scores represent skills deficits or performance deficits. Sample universal screening tools may be seen in the appendices. Evaluations of numerous tools are available at www.rti4success.org under the resource tab.

COLLABORATION

Collaboration with Response to Intervention involves a team of two or more professionals who share their expertise in order to implement instructional or behavioral strategies to benefit student learning.

Problem-Solving Team

The problem-solving team is a group of education professionals who collaborate together to consider student-specific data, brainstorm possible strategies/ interventions, and develop a plan of action to address a student-specific need.

Problem-Solving Approach to RTI

The problem-solving approach to RTI assumes that no given intervention will be effective for all students. RTI generally has four stages: problem identification, problem analysis, plan implementation, and plan evaluation. This approach to RTI is sensitive to individual student differences and depends on the integrity of implementing interventions.

There are five steps involved in this process:

Step 1: Collect and conduct ongoing assessment of data.

Step 2: Analyze assessed strengths and challenges to determine root causes.
   a. What have you observed?
   b. What information does the data provide?
   c. What are the strengths, challenges, and inferences?
   d. What is the root cause?

During this step of analysis, the team should look for dependent and independent variables. Identifying independent and dependent variables will guide the team in determining which elements may be influenced or modified by intervention.

Step 3: Establish SMART (specific, measureable, achievable, relevant and timely) goals. Set, review, and revise goals.

Step 4: Select scientifically research-based interventions.

Step 5: Progress monitor planned before, during, and after intervention.

This is a process very similar to PLCs or Data Teams used by many school districts across the country. A few items have been added to those steps to comply with the core principles of RTI, including universal screening, scientifically research-based intervention, and progress monitoring. Prior to moving students between tiers, the team should consider multiple data points of assessment. During the meeting, there is a focus on planning a time frame for and following through with appropriate assessments to set baselines and to monitor student progress.

Sample Team Meeting Minutes Form

Power Standard	
Today's Date:	Date of Next Meeting:
Success Criteria:	
Team Members Present: Facilitator: Note Taker: Data Technician: Time Keeper/Focus Monitor: Active Participants:	
Data Sources:	
Students Below Proficient	**Students Close to Proficient**
Students Proficient	**Students Above Proficient**
SMART Goal Percentage of _____ proficient and higher in specific standards will increase from _____ to _____ by _____, as measured by _____ given on _____.	Responsible for Progress Monitoring
Targeted Scientifically Research-based Interventions:	
Evaluation of the Response to the Above Intervention	
Have interventions been implemented with fidelity? ☐ Not implemented ☐ Partially implemented ☐ Fully implemented	
Student achievement results:	
Success indicators (evidence of actual impact on student learning):	
Reasons why interventions were or were not successful:	
Suggested adjustments or recommendations:	

Sample Data Analysis Form

Data Analysis	
Problem:	
Strengths:	**Inferences:**
Challenges:	**Inferences:**
Tier Level: Tier 1 – Universal Tier 2 – Targeted Tier 3 – Intensive	**Rationale:**
Interventions:	
Progress Monitoring Results:	

CHAPTER ONE

Tier 1 Scenarios

TIER 1 SNAPSHOT

What: Tier 1 core instruction is high-quality, research-based instruction provided to all students. Teachers provide differentiated instruction based on pre-assessed needs to ensure access to the curriculum for everyone in the class.

Who: Tier 1 instruction is provided by highly qualified general education teachers that provide quality research-based instruction.

Where: Instruction in Tier 1 typically takes place in the general education classroom.

When: Tier 1 instruction takes place during core direct instruction from the general educator.

Why: Approximately 80 to 90 percent of the students in Tier 1 should respond with proficiency to the high-quality instruction.

Keisha
Primary

(Writing)

Keisha is a very active five-year-old. She loves school, and her favorite subject is art. Keisha's mother is a receptionist at a local convalescent home, and her father is in the military currently serving overseas. Keisha has an older brother at the same school in the third grade.

Keisha is making good progress in kindergarten skills, but her teacher, Ms. Lymon, has noticed on the past few writing samples that Keisha and four other students in class are still struggling to write letters to form beginning words. Specifically, her formation is significantly behind her peers. Ms. Lymon feels that she must provide a specific strategy to help the students who are struggling so that a gap is not created as they move on to more advanced skills later in the school year.

> **Reflection:** *Keisha is only 5.2 years old. Do you think it is better for her teacher to wait until Keisha matures a bit more to begin differentiating instructional strategies? Why or why not?*

During the kindergarten/first-grade meeting, Ms. Lymon showed the team members the results of last week's writing sample and expressed concern that a few students still needed additional assistance. The following team members were present:

- Kindergarten teachers
- First-grade teachers
- Occupational therapist
- Academic coach

Notice that this was a combined K–1 grade-level team meeting. Some schools find it helpful to increase their ability to share through grade levels. Combined meetings may also be useful if there are only one or two teachers per grade level at a small school. Notice that on this particular team both an occupational therapist (OT) and an academic coach were present. The membership of teams will vary widely based on the needs of the students. There are a few students in the K–1 program who are receiving occupational therapy services in Keisha's school. The occupational therapist is on campus during the time of the bimonthly grade-level team meeting and often joins the group to collaborate on student needs. The K–1 team leader indicated that the input of related service providers has been invaluable. During the meeting the OT provided suggestions for those students who are not eligible for OT services but could benefit from specific strategies for developmental fine-motor coordination.

The grade-level team looked at all of the writing samples that Ms. Lymon and her colleagues collected. They began to professionally analyze the writing samples (see Exhibit 1.1). The team discussed Keisha's strengths and challenges and began making inferences about those strengths and challenges. Ms. Lymon indicated that Keisha and a few of her classmates do display proper sitting posture and pincer grasp, although a couple of students have indicated that their hands hurt after their writing assignment. The team mentioned that some students are grasping their pencils too tightly, as in Keisha's case, and the pencil lead breaks under the pressure.

The other kindergarten teacher displayed her student writing samples as well and saw the same issues with a few of her students. The occupational therapist asked both teachers to describe exactly how they are providing direct instruction on writing formation to the students. Both teachers indicated that they are using a lined chalkboard and reading a script from a writing handbook. The students are encouraged to copy from the whiteboard on to their papers as the teacher talks them through the process of forming the letters.

Before the team suggested possible strategies, one of the first-grade teachers asked if the vision records had been checked and were up-to-date for all of the students. She related a story from the last school year in which she struggled with a student new to the school for an entire semester before realizing that the student had eyeglasses but never wore them in class. Apparently, he accidently broke them and was afraid to tell his parents. The lesson is to remember Intervention Strategy 101: Always check health and sensory issues first; and Progress Monitoring 101: Document, document, document. It could indeed have saved time and frustration if the information regarding the glasses had been available to the new teacher. Ms. Lymon indicated that she had checked the records of all of her kindergarteners, and there was no indication at this point of health or sensory issues.

Exhibit 1.2 is a sample of some of the strategies that the team discussed. Remember that Tier 1 instructional strategies may prove helpful to all students and

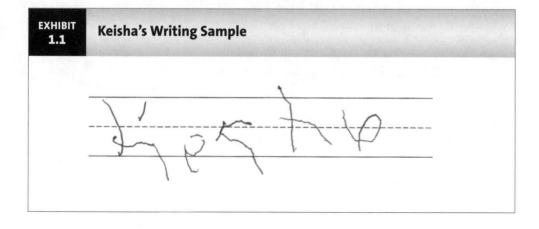

EXHIBIT 1.1 **Keisha's Writing Sample**

can be differentiated by the general educator as needed. Students in Tier 2 and Tier 3 may benefit from this instruction as well. They may, however, require additional time, more practice, a different modality, or a different type or method of presenting the direct instruction. The two kindergarten teachers said they would use one of the instructional strategies from the list shown in Exhibit 1.2 and report back to the committee at their next meeting in two weeks.

 IMPLEMENTATION TIP

The grade-level team discussed a variety of options based on their assessment shown in Exhibit 1.2. Here are additional items they discussed to help them decide on the implementation:

- ▶ **Interventions** may include time, such as duration and frequency (e.g., 20, 30, 45 minutes a day, two times a week, daily); environment (physical location, structure); personnel (teacher, specialist); and grouping (small 1:5 or 1:3, heterogeneous, homogenous). The higher the tier, the smaller the group and the formative assessment (two times a month, weekly, two times a week, daily). The higher the tier, the more frequent the need for assessment to monitor the student's progress. Remember, core Tier 1 provides the research-based instruction with differentiation as needed, based on the pre-assessed needs of the students from a highly qualified teacher during core instruction. Students in Tiers 2–3 require intensified intervention strategies and activities.

- ▶ **Strategies** shown are samples of the intentional adult actions that should have the greatest positive impact on student learning, such as the use of collaborative learning and nonlinguistic representations. Select the strategy based on the strengths, challenges, and inferences discussed during the meeting.

- ▶ **Activities** shown are the actions of the students, such as tracing in clay. The student tracing is the activity, but the strategy is the use of tactile objects.

NOTE: This is not intended to be an exhaustive list of possible activities and strategies for this area of content. Typically, there is not a dividing line between some of the tiers. It may be that the strategy or classroom activity will be appropriate for multiple tiers. In some cases, the time, intensity, and duration of a strategy

EXHIBIT 1.2 **Sample K–2 Writing**

Sample Tiers	Strategies and Activities	Description*
1, 2, 3	Provide proper writing instruments	Provide appropriate size and thickness of the writing instrument. A pencil grasp may also be used.
1, 2, 3	Provide ample time	Time should be available as an advance lesson (bell ringer) prior to the lesson, immediately following the class activity, or during a designated additional time, (e.g., 5–10 minutes of additional direct instruction and independent practice).
1, 2, 3	Trace over paper or on top of model letters	Student should lightly trace on top of preprinted letters on paper. Focus on the letters the student does not form correctly. Practice the correct form of one or more letters each day.
1, 2, 3	Trace over tactile surface	Trace letters on fine sandpaper, felt cutouts, shaving cream, or other tactile surface with finger and then with a pencil.
1, 2, 3	Trace on the student's back	Trace a letter with your finger (e.g., the letter K), on the student's back as you say the letter. Ask them to repeat the letter.
1, 2, 3	Trace in clay	Trace letters on soft clay with finger.
1, 2, 3	Use raised lines on paper	Paper with raised lines. Commonly used for students with visual impairments as well. Color-coded and start-stop symbol paper for primary grades.
1, 2, 3	Contrast colors on text or background	Use light-colored paper—pale pink, yellow, green, beige, etc.
1, 2, 3	Provide additional supervised practice	Provide direct supervised (one-on-one to one-on-three) observation of student practice. If necessary add a sheet of very fine sandpaper under the writing sheet to help with writing control.
1, 2, 3	Learning center/Learning stations	Provide writing prompts, tracing sheets, and ample opportunity for students to practice in a learning center (independent) or learning station (guided).
Additional:		
Additional:		
Additional:		

* Note: In most cases the general education teacher may provide the intervention/strategy described in the right-hand column. Additional interventionists may be available at the school to assist the teacher as needed.

Intervention strategies may vary. For example, Tier 2 intervention may be appropriate for a student in Tier 1 or 3, or a Tier 3 intervention strategy may be appropriate for Tier 2 as well. The decision about which strategy to use and it's time, duration, and frequency must be based on the analysis of the student needs.

Interventionists may include, but are not limited to, instructional coaches, literacy specialists, special education specialists, English Language Learner (ELL) specialists, paraprofessionals, training community volunteers such as from the Core of Retired Teachers, university students, related services personnel such as occupational/physical therapists, speech and language pathologists, and counselors or social workers. There are districts that describe this approach as "all hands on deck" to help the students. There have been individual discussions in school districts to determine who is qualified to provide the interventions. Typically, the licensed or certified professional should provide the direct instruction and all others may provide the continued guided practice. Some school districts restrict the use of special education and teachers of English Language Learners to only students on their caseload. There are many exceptions including, but not limited to, full inclusion classes where all students in class are taught in a collaborative model.

Source: House (2004)

may be modified to suit particular groups or individual students. Read the "How Does It Look" section to see which strategy, activity, and assessment was used by this particular team. Discuss other strategies that may be appropriate based on the scenario.

HOW DOES IT LOOK?

Following the grade-level team meeting, Ms. Lymon and the other kindergarten teacher and the two first-grade teachers decided that they would immediately implement two instructional strategies from the list of research-based strategies discussed in Exhibit 1.2. The next day, they gave four of their students, including Keisha, a handwriting paper with raised lines. They asked the students to feel the lines and then write lightly as they formed the letters. In Keisha's case, Ms. Lymon initially placed her hand on top of Keisha's to help her determine the amount of pressure required to form the letters. All four teachers asked the students to take their time and not rush through the letters. The teachers explained that they were looking for quality, not quantity. They gave three students, including Keisha, hand-held chalkboards on which the letters were written and explained the process as they went, encouraging the students to copy with air writing first, repeating the same instructions (e.g., up, down, around). They then asked the students to trace over each letter with their finger until the chalk disappeared. The students were watched initially to make sure that they practiced correctly. The remainder of the students completed the regular writing assignment, which proved positive for them, as each teacher worked with one to four students who required the additional (differentiated) instructional strategy.

The teachers also decided that they should use these instructional strategies for 10 minutes, three times a week, with three of the students who required Tier 2 targeted and Tier 3 intensive strategies. To make time for this activity, the teachers determined that using a learning station or preteaching (prior to the general group writing lesson) would be the best ways to accomplish this activity in order to ensure that students would have proper supervision and instruction.

HOW IS IT MONITORED?

The instructional goal that the grade-level team response set for the four students in each class was to improve in two weeks the students' ability to write on the line with age-appropriate formation. Determination of whether the goal was met would be based on collaborative observation of a written work sample.

The K–1 grade-level team agreed to reconvene in two weeks during their usual 45-minute meeting to review the work samples of the students and discuss next steps. At the next team meeting the K–1 teachers were prepared to collaboratively evaluate the work samples and decide whether to move the students to the next lesson. If students needed more help with the current area of instruction, the teachers would consider an additional instructional strategy or additional time, intensity, or duration of the current strategy.

Jimmy
Upper Elementary

(Note Taking)

Jimmy is a nine-year-old student at Eagle Elementary School. He lives with his mother. Jimmy often says that he likes being an only child but sometimes wishes he had an older brother to practice playing sports. He wants to be a famous football or baseball player.

Jimmy's mother is proud that he is doing so well in school and is really happy with the instruction he has had from all of the teachers. Lately, Jimmy's grades have been declining in social studies and science. These are new content courses for him that began in third grade. His teacher, Ms. Stevens, primarily uses lectures to convey information about science and social studies. Jimmy and his classmates try to keep up and take notes while she is talking. Approximately 80 percent of the students are successful in taking notes and performing well on her assessments, but a few students, including Jimmy, struggle to keep up. They frequently lose the content and miss the point of the lecture while trying to write. Jimmy does read the text on grade level, and that does help him. But Jimmy's mother is concerned that as he gets older this lecture style of presentation may be a problem for him through middle school and high school.

Jimmy's mother tries to help him at home, but is unclear what to do. She made an appointment with Jimmy's teacher. During the meeting Jimmy was present as well and expressed concern that he could not keep up with the lectures in class. Jimmy said he really likes social studies and science because his teacher always has fun hands-on homework assignments and activities at least once a week that he can participate in during class. He mentioned during the meeting that he feels that he is learning more through the models, demonstrations, and activities than through the teacher's 45-minute lectures (read from a teaching manual). Jimmy's mother asked to see Jimmy's grade-level achievement universal assessment scores in all of his academic classes so far this school year.

Jimmy's mother expressed alarm that his grades in science and social studies had slipped so low. According to the curriculum-based assessment, Jimmy's fall semester scores indicated that he began at the 3.3 grade level in science and social studies, but showed a decline to 2.7 by the winter semester. Jimmy's mother is also aware that this is the first time that Jimmy will be assessed in science on the state-mandated assessment and is worried that Jimmy may not pass on grade-level skills if the problem is not addressed right away. She said a lot of information about this new science assessment had been in the local newspaper lately. Jimmy's teacher, Ms. Stevens, was mentally taking note of a trend among several other fourth graders in her classroom as well. Many of her students appeared to be struggling with note taking. After reflecting for a few minutes, she told Jimmy's mother that she had a few ideas that could help Jimmy and should help many of the other students in her class as well.

Ms. Stevens said she would discuss her method of instruction with her colleagues and see if a few changes in her instructional methodology could help. She also made an assumption that note-taking skills had been previously taught in third grade.

> **Reflection:** *What immediate suggestions would you have for her lecture-style presentations? Why?*

After analyzing all of her students' social studies and science papers, Ms. Stevens found that their strengths were strong vocabulary skills, following directions, and average reading skills. Ms. Stevens decided that based on one of the students' biggest challenges, note taking, she would change her method of lecturing for two weeks and see how the students responded to the new instructional strategies. The next day, Ms. Stevens began with explicit direct instruction on note-taking skills. She also indicated that some of the students in class might need advance organizers or even nonlinguistic representations to take their notes.

Jimmy was excited about learning a strategy that could help him. But just before leaving with his mother he turned and asked Ms. Stevens one last question, "What if it doesn't work?" "Don't worry," Ms Stevens smiled. "We'll work together to make it work. I'm sure that the other fourth-grade teachers will share with me more ideas that have worked in their classrooms." She briefly explained to Jimmy and his mother that her school would have a formal meeting time every other week so that she could review student progress, analyze strengths and challenges, and implement instructional strategies to help all students. Ms. Stevens assured Jimmy and his mother that she would use a progress monitoring system that would help her keep a close eye on his progress.

Ms. Stevens spoke with her teammates about implementing the grade-level team meeting at their grade level and her team agreed to try the process. During the first grade-level team meeting for the fourth grade, Ms. Stevens shared the results of her initial informal assessments and instructional strategies. She also volunteered to be the fourth-grade team leader. After a discussion of the strengths and challenges of the fourth-grade students in science and social studies, the rest of the team decided to use the Tier 1 note-taking skills strategies and suggested a few other strategies for students in Tier 2 and Tier 3 as well. The first few team meetings were scheduled for 45 minutes, but they honestly took closer to an hour. Roles (team leaders, scribe/note taker, timekeeper, engaged participant, focus monitor) were quickly established, norms were agreed to, and the team immediately launched into the five-step meeting process described in the introduction on page xv. The instructional strategies the team discussed during their meeting are listed in Exhibit 1.3.

> **Reflection:** *Note taking and summarizing is listed as a skill in the fourth-grade standards for Jimmy's school district. Should his teacher still continue attempting strategies to teach him note taking or excuse him from that activity? Why or why not?*

IMPLEMENTATION TIP

The grade-level team discussed a variety of options based on their assessment shown in Exhibit 1.3. Here are additional items they discussed to help them decide on the implementation:

► **Interventions** may include time, such as duration and frequency (e.g., 20, 30, 45 minutes a day, two times a week, daily); environment (physical location, structure); personnel (teacher, specialist); and grouping (small 1:5 or 1:3, heterogeneous, homogenous). The higher the tier, the smaller the group and the formative assessment (two times a month, weekly, two times a week, daily). The higher the tier, the more frequent the need for assessment to monitor the student's progress. Remember, core Tier 1 provides the research-based instruction with differentiation as needed, based on the pre-assessed needs of the students from a highly qualified teacher during core instruction. Students in Tiers 2–3 require intensified intervention strategies and activities.

► **Strategies** shown are samples of the intentional adult actions that should have the greatest positive impact on student learning, such as the use of Cornell Notes (note taking and summarizing) and double-entry journals. Select the strategy based on the strengths, challenges, and inferences discussed during the meeting.

► **Activities** shown are the actions of the student, such as working with a study buddy.

NOTE: This is not intended to be an exhaustive list of possible activities and strategies for this area of content. Typically, there is not a dividing line between some of the tiers. It may be that the strategy or classroom activity will be appropriate for multiple tiers. In some cases, the time, intensity, and duration of a strategy may be modified to suit particular groups or individual students. Read the "How Does It Look" section to see which strategy, activity, and assessment was used by this particular team. Discuss other strategies that may be appropriate based on the scenario.

 HOW DOES IT LOOK?

The first day, Ms. Stevens began her science lesson in the following manner. First, she told the entire class that as part of the day's science lesson they would learn to take notes using Cornell Notes (see Appendix I). She provided a model of a completed form and preprinted the key "look for" words and content that would be used during her science presentation. For some of her students currently in Tier 2, Ms. Stevens also added a Cornell sheet with the key words preprinted in the left-hand column, with instructions to the students to "look and listen for" the key science

EXHIBIT 1.3 **Sample Note Taking**

Sample Tiers	Strategies and Activities	Description
1, 2, 3	Cornell Notes	Provide explicit instruction on this graphic organizer. Students are to write key vocabulary or content on the left side and fill in information on the right side of the graphic.
2, 3	Chunk the information	Provide short 3–7 minutes of information (provide visuals, vocabulary, demonstrations, or modeling as possible). Have students then interact with the information through notes, "think-pair-share," or choral cues. Choral cues are words that are repeated from the story or lecture.
2, 3	Notes review	Allow time between "chunks" of the lecture for students to review their notes independently or with a peer.
2, 3	Nonlinguistic representation	Use visuals, drawings, pictures, charts, graphic organizers, pictographs.
1, 2, 3	Vocabulary "look fors"	Write the vocabulary that students should "look or listen for" in advance of the lesson on the whiteboard or on their graphic organizer.
1, 2, 3	Shared notes	Students may review or share notes with a peer between "chunks" of information.
2, 3	Study buddy	At the beginning of class, students are paired with a homogeneous or heterogeneous partner that they can study with during class. During this time the students will share and discuss their notes with each other as the teacher monitors their work. (This is not the electronic Study Buddy product.)
3	Provide prewritten notes	Some students may experience difficulty with the ability to listen and write notes at the same time. Provide them with a transparency, buddy notes, or teacher's notes so that they can focus on the words or visuals presented during the lecture.
2, 3	Audiotape	Some academic content is available in audiotape format. The student can listen to the information multiple times in small segments if necessary.
2, 3	Videotape	Some academic content is available in videotape format. The student can watch and listen to the information multiple times in small segments, if necessary. Examples include, but are not limited to, *United Streaming* (Discovery Channel), the History Channel, PBS for Teachers, and Annenberg Media.
1, 2, 3	Advance organizers	There are numerous advance organizers (such as Cornell Notes or double-entry journals) to help students focus and organize information. Once students have learned the method of organizing information they can make their own organizers as well. A large variety of graphic organizers are available online.
1, 2, 3	Explicit direct instruction	A continuum of effective research-based strategies for increasing opportunities for learning by highly qualified teachers in the general education environment.
Additional:		
Additional:		
Additional:		

Sources: Marzano, 2001; Marzano, 2007; Carrell, 2007.

words during the segmented (chunked) lecture and to write the information in the right-hand column. The students in Tier 3 were given the opportunity to use nonlinguistic representations next to the preprinted Cornell Notes; a couple of students were given preprinted note pages so that they could use their auditory and visual skills to focus on the lesson. Keep in mind that students were given only what they needed based on the teacher's analysis. In your practice, you may provide direct instruction to all of your students in how to use each of the note-taking systems appropriate to the lesson and then allow students the opportunity to choose the one or ones that work best for them. Don't be surprised if they select nonlinguistic representations. Consider what is more important, their ability to absorb the content or the skill of note taking. Typically, students will self-select those strategies that they are most comfortable with if given the opportunity. However, if the skill of note taking is indeed crucial to your lesson, you may begin with the purpose, demonstration, exemplars, and exploratory practice to give students an opportunity to learn the skill in a manner that meets their learning style. For some students with learning disabilities, two or more cognitive activities presented simultaneously may prove challenging. The selection of prewritten or shared notes may be most appropriate.

Some students learn best by drawing images and listening, some by visual depiction, others by the physical motion of writing notes. Others may proclaim that they learn best by just listening, watching, or capturing only key words or symbols on paper. These and other learning-style differences apply to young students as well.

> **Reflection:** *Think of yourself or your former college mates. Have you heard people comment that it helps them to learn and to remember when they take notes, even if the professor has distributed written notes?*

Sometimes, teachers express concern that students will be unhappy that they are given different tools in a lesson. There is the concern of "fairness." Remind the students that they will be given what they need. For example, tell them, "If you need eyeglasses that's fine. You should be able to use them to help you see like everyone else. But your classmate sitting next to you can already see without glasses." Usually students quickly understand. Or use an example that would be more relevant for your students. But the key is to make it crystal clear that everyone in your class is important, and you refuse to sacrifice the needs of one student because someone else may see a difference in treatment. Your goal is to make sure that the needs of all students are being addressed.

It is extremely important to develop a positive relationship with the students and develop a warm, trusting, and inviting learning environment for everyone. Struggling students in particular will often look to things external to the class content for their peace of mind and motivation to learn. Frequently, it is the teacher who sets the tone and expectations for the class, including the belief that all students can learn. Students may learn at a different pace or in a different manner, but they can learn. Personally reflect on your classroom and evaluate if you have clearly established a positive learning environment in which students feel happy to support the learning of their classmates and feel comfortable expressing themselves in a mature manner. There may be times when you need to rely on the students coming forward and sharing with you what they feel they may need to do their best job.

Ms. Stevens, Jimmy's teacher, also decided that it might be a good idea to provide visuals and "chunk" the information in small segments of no more than five to seven minutes. At the end of each segment, she would check for understanding by asking the students to discuss in pairs or triads the following: What prior information does this remind you of? Compare or contrast the information. What is your opinion of what I just said? Share a similar story or idea. Repeat what I just said. Repeat key definitions in your own words with your partners. Review your notes with your partners. Fill in missing information with your partners.

HOW IS IT MONITORED?

Each of the fourth-grade teachers volunteered to provide two short common teacher-made assessments, maintain their own records of student progress, and report back to the grade-level team after a two-week period. The team noticed that student scores increased significantly following the implementation of the instructional strategies. They decided to continue using the advance organizers as an instructional strategy for all students who needed to use them during the segmented lectures. The students seemed to enjoy it, their scores improved, and the level of engagement was tremendous. Ms. Stevens discussed the idea of holding a team meeting on a bimonthly basis. The team used the skills shown on the Common Core State Standards to determine which pre-assessments to give. The fourth-grade teachers collaborated to compose the post-assessments. During each of their bimonthly meetings, they followed the five grade-level team steps with fidelity and checked to make sure that students were responding as expected to the instructional strategies and meeting their goals.

Brianna
Secondary

(Spelling)

Brianna is an athletic student who enjoys all types of sports. She plays sports both at school and in her community. She is a solid "B" student. She hopes to become either a professional athlete or a veterinarian when she finishes school. On most weekends, Brianna is practicing soccer or basketball or volunteering her time in the vet's office.

Brianna's favorite academic subjects are mathematics and science. Her neighborhood veterinarian indicated that skills in both mathematics and science are important if she intends to pursue a career as a vet. Brianna is very concerned about her writing skills and realizes proper spelling is important as well. When writing assignments are required for class, Brianna struggles with organization of her work, spelling, and punctuation. She often jokes with her friends that her spelling in Spanish class is better than her spelling in English because the words seem to be spelled the way they sound in Spanish. Brianna keeps an electronic English dictionary with her at all times. It is a pocket Webster version that she purchased at the school bookstore. It does help her because she can hear a word to make sure she has selected the correct word, and she can listen to the definition as well. It seems that her biggest problem right now is being able to complete the work in each of her classes quickly, without multiple spelling errors.

Brianna's English teacher has tried to help Brianna by providing additional time for her class and homework assignments. It seems to take her almost twice as much time as the other students as she patiently looks up so many words. It is becoming increasingly more frustrating for her. Brianna has a good vocabulary, but her spelling is so poor she is graded down, and her grade point average is beginning to drop.

Brianna tries to rely on the computer to help catch her errors but notices that it does not help with all of her errors, such as homonyms. Unfortunately, the amount of time that it takes Brianna to look up individual words and complete assignments has caused her mother to reduce the amount of time that Brianna is allowed to participate in other extracurricular activities after school. She must also maintain her grade point average in order to continue to compete in sports. Brianna indicated to her mother that she believes "it's not fair" because she feels that spelling was not actually taught in her classes. After a review of the records and discussions with the previous teachers, it was reported that the students did have spelling lessons integrated into their core content classes. But the program was not planned as a team, and integration of spelling was conducted with mixed results.

Several ninth-grade teachers at Brianna's school had noticed the poor spelling skills of the freshmen students, despite the fact that the students are intelligent and eager. One teacher also noticed that these students had strong vocabulary as well, but the spelling seemed to stunt their proficiency scores in writing. The content department team (leaders for all core content areas for the ninth grade) decided to hold a joint meeting on Wednesday afternoon at 3:30 pm. They agreed to conduct business for one hour. In order to accomplish their goal of completing all five steps of the meeting process referred to in the introduction, they agreed to bring a common writing sample for their students as well as the assessment tools they used to score the work. The language arts department chair volunteered to be the team leader of the multidisciplinary core team. The day of the meeting, the team analyzed the common spelling errors of most of the students across disciplines. After careful analysis and determining the root cause, they created a list of possible instructional strategies that could be appropriate for the general education classroom. All of the content leaders decided to focus on two strategies for the next two weeks in order to begin improving the spelling skills for the ninth graders. The first plan was to create a list of the crucial words teachers used in each of their classes based on the Common Core State Standards. The second strategy was to use words from the books of lists for mathematics, social studies, and science. The language arts teacher also decided to use the *Writing Teacher's Book of Lists* (Muschla, 2004) so that all students would have a common core of spelling words for their discipline. Rather than using the elementary "word wall," the team agreed to create a visual thesaurus, which would allow students to learn more than one word at a time associated with the content. The science and mathematics department leaders indicated that they would prefer using double-entry journals that students could maintain that would include the word, a nonlinguistic representation, and an example of how the word is used. They wanted to intentionally integrate the spelling lesson into their normal teaching practice but have students emphasize the spelling with a closer review of the rules of spelling structures so they could confidently spell the content words with accuracy. The spelling strategies and activities shown in Exhibit 1.4 are examples of the strategies considered by the content department team during their discussion of the student's individual needs.

IMPLEMENTATION TIP

The ninth-grade English department team discussed a variety of options based on their assessment shown in Exhibit 1.4. Here are additional items they discussed to help them decide on the implementation:

- ▶ **Interventions** may include time, such as duration and frequency (e.g., 20, 30, 45 minutes a day, two times a week, daily); environment (physical location, structure); personnel (teacher, specialist); and grouping (small 1:5 or 1:3, heterogeneous, homogenous). The higher the tier, the smaller the group and the formative assessment (two times a month, weekly, two times a week, daily). The higher the tier, the more frequent the need for assessment to monitor the student's progress. Remember, core Tier 1 provides the research-based instruction with differentiation as needed, based on the pre-assessed needs of the students from a highly qualified teacher during core instruction. Students in Tiers 2–3 require intensified intervention strategies and activities.

- ▶ **Strategies** shown are samples of the intentional adult actions that should have the greatest positive impact on student learning, such as direct instruction of explicit spelling rules. Select the strategy based on the strengths, challenges, and inferences discussed during the meeting.

- ▶ **Activities** shown are the actions of the student, such as highlighting root words.

NOTE: This is not intended to be an exhaustive list of possible activities and strategies for this area of content. Typically, there is not a dividing line between some of the tiers. It may be that the strategy or classroom activity will be appropriate for multiple tiers. In some cases, the time, intensity, and duration of a strategy may be modified to suit particular groups or individual students. Read the "How Does It Look" section to see which strategy, activity, and assessment was used by this particular team. Discuss other strategies that may be appropriate based on the scenario.

Reflection: *Brianna is beginning to express opposition to activities that are centered on spelling. She is convinced that the only thing she needs is the computer's spell checker. What would you say to her?*

EXHIBIT 1.4	Sample Spelling	

Sample Tiers	Strategies and Activities	Description
1, 2, 3	Graphic organizer	Dissect the word, (i.e., root word, part of speech, syllables for key words).
2, 3	Highlight root words	Underline root words in pencil or highlighter.
1, 2, 3	Explicit spelling rules	Consistently practice a spelling rule, such as "*i* before *e* except after *c*." Practice prefix and suffix. Post-assess. When a rule is mastered, a new one is introduced.
1, 2, 3	Devlop a spelling thesaurus	When a new topic is introduced, students can create a visual thesaurus. See Exhibit 1.5.
1, 2, 3	Entrance/exit slip	Students will use a few minutes of class responding to a very short assessment of the spelling words every two days or once a week.
1, 2, 3	Physical practice (repetition)	Some students need to write the words several times.
2, 3	Mnemonics	Practice mnemonic rhymes, phrases, and illustrations that assist in remembering.
Additional:		
Additional:		
Additional:		

Sources: House, 2004; Marzano, 2007

The next group of words the teachers focused on were word categories, such as synonyms, adjectives, and transition words. The leaders decided to ask every ninth-grade teacher in their department to write a set of words on a poster board, whiteboard, or chart paper every week. The exemplars that teachers posted were designed to help enhance the students' ability to use their growing spelling skills more fluently. Commercial online thesauruses can be found on Web sites such as www.visualthesaurus.com. Exhibit 1.5 represents a sample of the student-made thesaurus. The student-made thesaurus can be drawn individually in a notebook or on a classroom wall using poster paper.

EXHIBIT 1.5   **Student-Made Thesaurus**

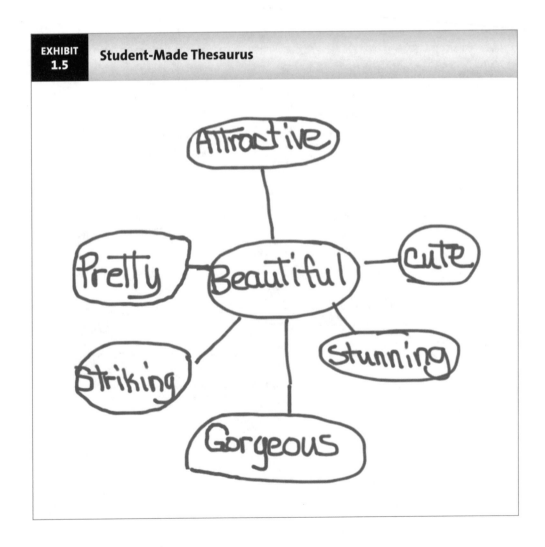

HOW DOES IT LOOK?

The core ninth-grade teachers agreed to discuss key elements of the targeted content-specific words for their discipline with their students. They began the first two weeks with root words. The content department team agreed that at the beginning of each class session three days a week for two weeks, they would begin their bell ringer or warm-up activity with an introduction to the key spelling words, which will be covered later in class using explicit instruction. The students would be given ample opportunity to practice the words throughout the period. Students would then be given a short assessment in the form of an exit slip. Teachers would be explicit in their direct instruction to make sure students understood that the purpose of the activity was to increase spelling skills in their content area. Students would have to demonstrate their ability to spell the new words correctly at the end of each week in sentences appropriate for each content discipline. This activity would take approximately five to seven minutes of class time three times each week. The students would be allowed in some cases to correct their own papers or to have peer corrections and submit the papers before the end of the hour. Students who are proficient spellers would be given alternative assignments during the seven minutes of instruction if necessary.

HOW IS IT MONITORED?

The teachers of ninth-grade students agreed to collaborate by department on their spelling instruction on a weekly basis. Each teacher agreed to keep a record of the successes and challenges with specific students based on the weekly exit slips. The teachers met within their departments two weeks later after trying their spelling instructional strategy to report whether or not they saw students responding appropriately to the strategy; their goal was 80 percent. Approximately 85 percent responded with 95 to 100 percent accuracy to the instructional strategy selected by the team for the first two weeks.

The results were positive, so the team decided to continue this strategy as a weekly part of their core instruction to help increase acquisition of new content vocabulary and spelling skills. They decided to continue a minimum of three times a week and to reassess their progress every two weeks. Their goal was to close the gap for the 15 percent of students who required strategies in Tier 2 and Tier 3. Examples of some of the strategies they discussed for these students may be seen in Exhibit 1.4.

Their intention was to continue working with students so that by the end of the school year all the students would enter the tenth grade with proficient spelling skills.

Students receiving Tier 2 targeted assistance would have a reduction in the number of words to be spelled but with a focus on additional practice or the spelling rule associated with the categories of words to be learned. The time would increase from five to seven minutes to a full 10 minutes three times a week for a total of 30 minutes a week as needed. Remember, the words were all content specific so that the students could continue with the general class lesson. Students would also have the opportunity to work with a peer (study buddy/partner) and use a graphic organizer to help dissect the words into roots, syllables, and parts of speech. Students in Tier 3 would receive intensive intervention. First, the students would be provided with Tier 2 graphic organizers along with an opportunity to work with an interventionist. The interventionist would work within the course content to provide assistance for the student by highlighting words, breaking words into syllables, using visualization of words in context, using color codes, and tracing over the words with a pencil as the student verbalized chunks of the word. To increase memory of a long list of words where the spelling has been learned, students could be taught to use an appropriate form of mnemonics as well. These are strategies that the interventionist might use when students do not respond as expected to the Tier 1 or Tier 2 instructional strategies.

HOW HAVE YOU THOUGHT ABOUT?

Teachers in the upper elementary and secondary grades often encounter students who struggle with linguistic skills in writing and spelling. Some students need additional support in organization, especially with note taking in core content classes. General education teachers should be aware of and implement the best instructional practices for differentiation in the classroom.

As you reflect on the three students in Tier 1, think about how their situation applies to your teaching and learning. Consider these questions:

► What additional intervention strategies have you used in your classroom that has proven successful for students who struggle with writing skills?

► How could you design different homework assignments to support improvement in note taking and summarization?

► What type of technology could be used to strengthen writing and spelling skills?

CHAPTER TWO

Tier 2 Scenarios

 TIER 2 SNAPSHOT

What: Tier 2 instructional intervention is high-quality, research-based core instruction, plus targeted supplemental instruction based on assessed and closely monitored student progress.

Who: Tier 2 instructional intervention may be provided by a highly qualified general-education teacher who models quality research-based instruction or another licensed professional, such as an instructional coach or specialist.

Where: Instruction in Tier 2 typically takes place in the general-education classroom. In a few cases students are pulled out for specific training as needed.

When: Intensity of the time, duration and frequency of the targeted instructional intervention, and progress monitoring may be increased as determined by the grade level or content discipline team based on the pre-assessed needs of the student.

Why: Approximately 10 to 15 percent of the students who do not respond as expected to Tier 1 core instruction may require supplemental small group assistance.

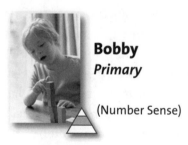

Bobby
Primary

(Number Sense)

Bobby is a very energetic young student. He is always moving and touching things. Even in his seat he is constantly squirming and moving about. Ms. Frankis has used a number of strategies to help Bobby focus his attention on academic activity. She noticed that Bobby and two other classmates struggle with number sense. Specifically, Bobby uses

21

random numbers when counting or explaining things. He points to and counts manipulatives two, and sometimes three, times before moving on to the next one. Ms. Frankis said he can skip count verbally to music or count to 50 with his classmates, but when asked to perform alone he goes back to randomly selecting numbers.

The first thing Ms. Frankis did was to check with the school nurse to see if there was perhaps an auditory or visual problem that she should know about. Nurse Grayson said the records from Bobby's father indicated Bobby is in excellent health and has good vision and hearing. Bobby did not attend preschool and is new to the community, so she decided to contact the father to ask about his activities at home. Bobby's father mentioned that Bobby likes to sing and repeat things but has not really noticed his use of numbers in any particular context.

Bobby's father said that he is a long-distance truck driver and is frequently away from home for months at a time. His wife left the family six months ago, and he moved to this community to be closer to Bobby's grandmother, who is currently the primary caregiver. Bobby's father has four children, and he indicated that his job on the road is the only way he can keep food on the table. He is willing to keep in contact with the teacher but feels that Bobby's paternal grandmother should be contacted for more information or to answer any questions. After a discussion with Bobby's grandmother, Ms. Frankis said that she would share with her next week the results of the Data Team meeting. His grandmother offered to practice a few minutes each evening with Bobby at home.

> **Reflection:** *If you had the opportunity to interview Bobby's grandmother, what questions would you ask her?*

Ms. Frankis decided to discuss Bobby's assessments with her grade-level team. She had tried numerous Tier 1 instructional strategies to help Bobby with number sense and was concerned about letting too much more time go by without finding an appropriate intervention that would yield a successful response. When Ms. Frankis met with her grade-level team, she said that her general methods of teaching her kindergarten students basic number sense worked for at least 80 to 85 percent of her students. Typically, she introduces new numbers by counting objects in the room and using workbook activities, number songs, and a large wall chart depicting numbers 1 to 100.

After meeting with her colleagues on the kindergarten team and explaining the problem, several of her colleagues reported that they had similar problems with teaching these skills. They also reported that they have a few students this school year who are still struggling. One team member mentioned a need for maturity on the part of the student. Ms. Frankis replied that that may be true, but she expressed concern that the gap would continue to grow if she didn't take immediate steps to intervene.

The team analyzed strengths, challenges, inferences, and root causes of the problem and produced a small list of intervention strategies (Exhibit 2.1) that could be used to help Bobby and a few other students. They decided to immediately introduce two interventions the next day. One strategy would be to provide enlarged tactile counters for kinesthetic manipulation. The second strategy would be to allow for a second rotation of practice with the general education teacher during math class.

> **Reflection:** *If the use of tactile counters and kinesthetic manipulatives does not produce the expected results for Bobby, what else might you suggest to the team?*

IMPLEMENTATION TIP

The grade-level team discussed a variety of options based on their assessment shown in Exhibit 2.1. Here are additional items they discussed to help them decide on the implementation:

▶ **Interventions** may include time, such as duration and frequency (e.g., 20, 30, 45 minutes a day, two times a week, daily); environment (physical location, structure); personnel (teacher, specialist); and grouping (small 1:5 or 1:3, heterogeneous, homogenous). The higher the tier, the smaller the group and the formative assessment (two times a month, weekly, two times a week, daily). The higher the tier, the more frequent the need for assessment to monitor the student's progress. Remember, core Tier 1 provides the research-based instruction with differentiation as needed, based on the pre-assessed needs of the students from a highly qualified teacher during core instruction. Students in Tiers 2–3 require intensified intervention strategies and activities.

▶ **Strategies** shown are samples of the intentional adult actions that should have the greatest positive impact on student learning, such as the use of kinesthetic activities. Select the strategy based on the strengths, challenges, and inferences discussed during the meeting.

▶ **Activities** shown are the actions of the student. In this case the student seems to learn best through gross motor movement. The activities may include the use of arms, legs, or the whole body to respond to various prompts.

NOTE: This is not intended to be an exhaustive list of possible activities and strategies for this area of content. Typically, there is not a dividing line between some of the tiers. It may be that the strategy or classroom activity will be appropriate for multiple tiers. In some cases, the time, intensity, and duration of a strategy may be modified to suit particular groups or individual students. Read the "How Does It Look" section to see which strategy, activity, and assessment was used by this particular team. Discuss other strategies that may be appropriate based on the scenario.

EXHIBIT 2.1	Sample Number Sense	
Sample Tiers	**Strategies and Activities**	**Description**
1, 2, 3	Tactile counters	Counting blocks or tangible manipulatives that students can move around in various groups.
2, 3	Extend guided practice	Give students more time and multiple opportunities to interact with the numbers in a variety of settings so that they will recognize the similarities and relationship of numbers to context.
2, 3	Color code patterned numbers	Numbers may be color coded by patterns such as multiples of twos, threes, etc.
2, 3	Kinesthetic activity	Allow students to, for example, hop as they count, stretch and pretend to be numbers, hold up number cards, and move around to manipulate the cards in order and in patterned groups.
Additional:		
Additional:		
Additional:		

Source: Stein, Silbert, and Carnine, 1997.

HOW DOES IT LOOK?

The next day, Ms. Frankis and her fellow kindergarten teachers embarked on their new intervention strategy. They used large tactile counters the size of building blocks so that students could take the time to actually feel the singularity of the counters before moving on. Initially, students discussed how the counters felt: smooth, rough, soft, bumpy, and so on. Then they moved on to count the blocks, taking their time to work for accuracy as they lifted each block and understood that every number they touched was important. Next, the students associated the number with the written number. Each block had a large tactile number imprinted on it as well.

The kindergarten teachers felt that more time would be needed to use their intervention strategy at least three times a week. They decided to use a university tutor for an extra 10 minutes a day for a total of 50 minutes per week. First, direct instruction in the form of a workstation lesson rotation was provided to those students who required targeted assistance. The kindergarten students loved the relationship they developed with their tutors. Ms. Frankis also mentioned that the physical movement and manipulation of the larger blocks stimulated Bobby's constant desire to touch things and to move around. Now he could move and learn at the same time. Sometimes, tutors sat next to students, and at other times, if the activity was too loud or disruptive for others in the class, tutors and students sat on the floor in the hall just outside of the classroom. It was a great match for the teacher and for the students.

HOW IS IT MONITORED?

The teachers on the grade-level team for kindergarten agreed to monitor the progress of each of their students in Tier 2 (including Bobby) by providing an informal assessment on a biweekly basis. The assessment was an observation of the student's ability to proficiently count in succession with and without manipulatives with 100 percent accuracy. The teachers started with one to four small numbers then added two more at the beginning of each week. They continued to reinforce the numbers in different contexts throughout the day. For example, students counted how many chairs, students, pencils, books, crayons, and so on, were inside and outside the classroom. As a result, students could see the connection between the new numbers and their environment.

Even though this intervention strategy seemed to be successful, it was important for the teachers to document what they observed and to be able to report to their colleagues in two weeks. They decided on two documentation methods. One was a time chart that documented the additional time provided each week to each student in Tier 2. The second method was to ask the cross-grade tutors to keep a small graph of students' progress during the practice sessions. Ms. Frankis and her colleagues monitored the student graphs daily and spoke to the tutors once a week. In two weeks, all of the kindergarten teachers reported back to their content department team members and discovered that Bobby and his Tier 2 classmates had made tremendous progress. The teachers were close to their goal of 100 percent proficiency, and they agreed to continue the intervention strategy for the next two months to close that gap even further. Bobby and his classmates would also continue with the same direct instruction strategies being used for his classmates in Tier 1 along with the use of tactile and kinesthetic manipulatives but without the use of cross-grade tutors.

Ms. Frankis did express concern, however, about another student in Bobby's class who even after using the Tier 2 intervention strategies was still below expectation. The team decided to try another strategy with the instructional coach for two weeks and to obtain her feedback before considering a move to Tier 3 for that student. He could continue with the fourth-grade tutor; they had developed a very positive relationship, and it was evident that his attitude about mathematics had changed in a positive manner. The team could definitely see progress, but not yet 100 percent proficient as anticipated. The team decided to also request the assistance of the mathematics coach one day a week to push-in (work) inside the classroom. The coach would provide a 15-minute segment one time a week and would report back to the team in two weeks to share the progress and see if the time or method needed to be modified to meet the students' needs.

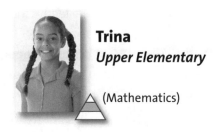

Trina
Upper Elementary

(Mathematics)

Trina is a shy yet enthusiastic fourth-grade student. She was born in Louisiana, but her family has moved numerous times due to a disaster in her hometown a few years ago. Economic hardships have befallen the family. There have been brief periods of time when the entire family lived in their automobile. Trina has one older brother, age 13, and a younger sister, age 5. Her mother works part-time at a local discount store, and her father is out of work. In his spare time, he tries to help his children acclimate to each new school. His trade is carpentry, and he is hoping to find employment soon.

Due to the numerous moves, Trina has several gaps in her education, but she is not eligible for special education services. The school psychologist reminded the team of the eligibility requirements for students being considered for special education as defined by Specific Learning Disability (Child with a Disability, Rules and Regulations [2004]) and suggested that they work together to provide intervention strategies specific to Trina's needs.

Reflection: *Do you think Trina should be referred to the special education department again for testing? Why or why not? Provide information from the scenario to defend your position.*

Trina is currently a grade below chronological grade level according to the universal screening given to Trina three weeks after her arrival at her new school. The reading comprehension score was 3.5, and the writing was 3.3, both within the average range. Her mathematics score in basic computation, however, was 2.8, an area of concern for Trina's teacher. Her teacher is convinced that the mathematics score can improve, and she is eager to provide smaller, informal, teacher-made assessments to zero in on the core problems so that she can track Trina's progress prior to the winter universal assessment.

Trina's teacher last year indicated that he felt he was close to a strong plan of action for targeted assistance to help Trina when the family abruptly moved out of state. When she arrived the third week at her new school, Trina's new teacher, Ms. Jamison, immediately gave her the district's universal screening. Fortunately, the assessments in reading, writing, and mathematics were short and easy to score, providing the teacher with immediate feedback that would help form her initial instruction.

It was clear that Trina was operating below grade level and would need additional assistance. Ms. Jamison's goal was to intervene early so that the academic gap would not widen. For three weeks, Ms. Jamison carefully watched Trina's slow progress as she labored with her math lessons. Her teacher tried differentiating instruction by giving Trina more time, cooperative learning activities, and a Fast Math computer program, but her progress was still very slow. Her informal assessment results indicated that she was not responding as expected to the Tier 1 core instruction along with her grade-level peers. During the next grade-level meeting, Ms. Jamison discussed a common formative assessment that would target the specific skills that the students were currently working on in class. Ms. Jamison is a highly qualified teacher and is delighted to have Trina in class. She is eager to help Trina reach proficiency or higher. She plans to use all of her professional skills and resources to that end.

The fourth-grade grade-level team met the next day at 7:30 a.m. (classes start at 8:45 a.m.). Ms. Jamison shared her class's fourth-grade math test scores, which now included Trina's, with her colleagues on the grade-level team. The team facilitator (team leader) indicated that at this point all students should be proficient in division problems. She suggested that the team discuss the students' strengths and challenges, make inferences, and determine the root causes of the problems experienced by the students (approximately 20 percent) who were not responding as expected to the Tier 1 core instructional strategies for this particular mathematics skill.

After careful analysis, the team noticed that several of the students, including Trina, had splintered skills or gaps in their instruction. It was their belief that one part of the root cause was poor place value, regrouping, and number sense skills. It was clear from the numerous work samples that the teachers brought to the team meeting that the students knew the basic math facts of addition, subtraction, and multiplication of single digits but lacked the understanding of how and when to use these basic facts in operation. The fourth-grade team decided to use explicit (alternative) preteaching through direct instruction with graphic models. Students also used a double-entry math journal during 15-minute station teaching in class. A list of additional intervention strategies is shown in Exhibit 2.2.

IMPLEMENTATION TIP

The grade-level team discussed a variety of options based on their assessment shown in the exhibit below. Here are additional items they discussed to help them decide on the implementation:

- ► **Interventions** may include time, such as duration and frequency (e.g., 20, 30, 45 minutes a day, two times a week, daily); environment (physical location, structure); personnel (teacher, specialist); and grouping (small 1:5 or 1:3, heterogeneous, homogenous). The higher the tier, the smaller the group and the formative assessment (two times a month, weekly, two times a week, daily). The higher the tier, the more frequent the need for assessment to monitor the student's progress. Remember, core Tier 1 provides the research-based instruction with differentiation as needed, based on the pre-assessed needs of the students from a highly qualified teacher during core instruction. Students in Tiers 2–3 require intensified intervention strategies and activities.

- ► **Strategies** shown in the chart below are samples of the intentional adult actions that should have the greatest positive impact on student learning, such as the use of alternative instruction (pre-teaching). Select the strategy based on the strengths, challenges, and inferences discussed during the meeting.

- ► **Activities** shown in the chart below are the actions of the students, such as drawing representations of math problems in a journal as a reminder.

NOTE: This is not intended to be an exhaustive list of possible activities and strategies for this area of content. Typically, there is not a dividing line between some of the tiers. It may be that the strategy or classroom activity will be appropriate for multiple tiers. In some cases, the time, intensity, and duration of a strategy may be modified to suit particular groups or individual students. Read the "How Does It Look" section to see which strategy, activity, and assessment was used by this particular team. Discuss other strategies that may be appropriate based on the scenario.

EXHIBIT 2.2   **Sample Mathematics**

Sample Tiers	Strategies and Activities	Description
1, 2, 3	Alternative preteaching	Students requiring targeted or intensive instruction may be gathered in a small group prior to the class lesson for 3 to 4 minutes to discuss new math vocabulary, review problem solving. The remainder of the class may complete an entrance slip or bell ringer/warm-up activity.
2, 3	Direct instruction	A continuum of effective research-based strategies for increasing opportunities for learning by highly qualified teachers in the general education environment.
2, 3	Station teaching	Students rotate in small groups to a variety of learning stations, including one that includes direct instruction from the teacher.
2, 3	Tutoring	Tutoring may be presented before, during, or after school. The team should determine the time, duration, and intensity of the tutoring. It should be a second or third dose to supplement the core instruction.
1, 2, 3	Double entry journal	In this example, the student will write the mathematics problem in the left column or page and solve the problem in digits and words or nonlinguistic representations.
1, 2, 3	Computerized math programs	Research-based computerized math programs are available at the What Works Clearinghouse at http://ies.ed.gov/ncee/wwc/
2, 3	Additional guided practice time	Additional guided practice time may last 7–15 minutes or 15–30 minutes based on student need. This can be done before or after class, during station rotation, flex time, or with a push-in interventionist during class.
Additional:		
Additional:		
Additional:		

Source: U.S. Department of Education, Institute of Education Sciences, What Works Clearinghouse at http://ies.ed.gov/ncee/wwc/

HOW DOES IT LOOK?

Ms. Jamison was very motivated to help get her students in Tier 2, including Trina, back on track as quickly as possible. She enlisted the help of a volunteer retired teacher to participate in a system that would provide students with an opportunity to rotate in learning stations in small homogenous groups. Students rotated to Ms. Jamison for direct instruction, to the retired teacher for guided practice, and then on to independent practice. On days when the retired teacher was not available, Ms. Jamison included a computer software program as one of the rotation stations. All students rotated through, but the type of instruction Ms. Jamison provided to each group was differentiated to meet their learning needs. In Trina's group, for example, manipulatives were used as Ms. Jamison provided direct instruction to help the students with regrouping. This process of station teaching was specifically scheduled for 15 minutes daily. In the station rotation with Ms. Jamison, Trina and her peers were shown how to use the double-entry journal to record and solve their math problems. The students were required to maintain a double-entry journal of all new math problems and to complete at least two problems during each session with 100 percent proficiency.

Ms. Jamison was most excited about providing Trina with the double-entry journal because she felt confident that it would be an asset to Trina in the event that her family moved again in the middle of the school year. Ms. Jamison told Trina that the journal was her private "math strategies journal" that would help her remember the math strategies that she'd learned in Ms. Jamison's classroom. During the remaining class time, students used the skills they'd learned in their small groups to complete differentiated assignments. Along with rotating through the learning stations, the students in Tier 3 intensive were also assigned to a short session with the mathematics software program at least once each week.

 ## HOW IS IT MONITORED?

Ms. Jamison and her colleagues on the fourth-grade team decided to use the progress monitoring form in Exhibit 2.3 to document the response to the mathematics interventions shown above. Students in Tier 2 were responding as predicted. The grade-level team decided to continue the model with a grade-level team review every two weeks as they moved forward on their pacing guide for academic standards until the next universal assessment in January.

EXHIBIT 2.3   **Progress Monitoring Report Form**

Response to Intervention

Initial date: _____

Name of Student: _____ Birth date: _____ Age: _____

Specify target or intensive group: _____

List names:

School: _____

District: _____ Grade: _____

City: _____ State: _____

Progress Monitor: _____

Position: _____

1. What is the problem? (Assessment/date):

2. Which research-based intervention will be monitored? (based on team analysis):

3. Which method(s) and what frequency will be used to progress monitor?

☐ Assessment scores: _____
   (Name/results/dates)

☐ Administrative walk-through/sweeps: _____
   (Dates and times)

☐ Observations: _____
   (Frequency/class/dates/time)

☐ Interviews: _____
   (Name[s])

☐ Data Team/PLC: _____
   (Date/results)

Universal screening results (Fall): _____

Universal screening results (Winter): _____

Universal screening results (Spring): _____

Behavior notes:

EXHIBIT 2.3 | **Progress Monitoring Report Form** *(continued)*

Student/Group _____

Progress monitoring data:

Baseline   Intervention

Baseline results:

Monitoring intervals: ☐ Daily ☐ Biweekly ☐ Weekly ☐ Bimonthly ☐ Monthly

Ref. #	Monitoring narrative (date/results):	Determine effectiveness or need for further change in intensity, time, or resources (date/results)

EXHIBIT 2.3   **Progress Monitoring Report Form** *(continued)*

Progress Monitoring Team Analysis

Student(s):

Problem Statement:	
Strengths:	Inferences:
Challenge/Weakness:	Inferences:
Root cause:	

All Interventions must be provided with fidelity

Tier 1	Universal	Provide high-quality scientifically research-based instruction and differentiation of content, process, or product in general education. This applies to all students based on their individual needs.
Tier 2	Targeted	General education instruction of Tier 1 plus specialized intervention that includes consideration of small group, specific minutes per day or week lasting approximately 30 minutes each session.
Tier 3	Intensive	Students who did not respond to Tier 2 interventions require intensive instruction that includes increased frequency, duration, and smaller groups, sometimes 1:1.

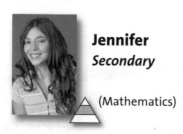

Jennifer
Secondary

(Mathematics)

Jennifer really likes school. She is very popular and keeps up with all of her friends on Twitter and Facebook. She likes to play games and chat with pals on Skype. Jennifer is an average reader and likes to read mystery stories, "hang out" at the mall with friends, and go to movies. School is a positive experience for her, but she is struggling with her math class. She has poor math fact skills and often exclaims with frustration, "I just can't see it!" Jennifer's teacher, Mr. Gibbs, asked her to use the calculator to solve some of the math problems only to discover that she was unsure which numbers to put into the calculator. Her biggest concern is how to complete word problems. She finds the multiple steps and the math vocabulary confusing. By the time she gets to the end of the word problem, she is unsure what to do with all the numbers.

Mr. Gibbs tried a number of universal strategies, which improved Jennifer's scores a little but not significantly enough to help her catch up to her classmates. One of the intervention strategies that Mr. Gibbs tried was to reduce the number of problems, which allowed her a little more time to complete each problem. He explained to her that the focus would be on accuracy, not quantity. She was also given a calculator to help her solve problems, but this yielded very little success, as mentioned above. It occurred to Mr. Gibbs that the use of a calculator was premature. There were more concrete skills he needed to teach first with direct instruction. The result of Jennifer's universal mathematics screening indicated that she is below proficient and should be targeted for additional intervention (Tier 2). Mr. Gibbs is concerned about Jennifer's math issues and realizes there is urgency to help her before she moves to the next grade. He also firmly believes that with the proper intervention, he can help Jennifer as well as a few other students in the class use a step-by-step approach to word-problem solutions.

During the mathematics department team meeting at Skylar High School, Mr. Gibbs and his colleagues shared their current class scores for basic-operation word problems. While reviewing the math data, Mr. Gibbs pointed out a particular concern about Jennifer and seven other students in his second-hour math class of 38 students. He shared the strategies that he had tried so far but admitted that it was not really working. The gap was getting wider. The team agreed that they must act immediately to help the students. He is pressed for time and has 30 other students to consider.

> **Reflection:** *What do you think Mr. Gibbs can do? Should he leave Jennifer and her peers behind and move on with the rest of his students? Fail the lagging students this year and just have them repeat the grade next year? What would you do?*

The decision of the math department team was to analyze the strengths and challenges of all the students who presented issues similar to those described in Jennifer's profile. The team determined that interventions needed to take place immediately to help the students in this group. Interventions included the use of an advance organizer to help guide students through the process of solving the word problems. Students in Tier 2 would also be asked to use a composition book to develop a strategies notebook with highlighted or underlined vocabulary essential to the math problem-solving process. Mr. Gibbs mentioned to the team that he felt he had prematurely provided the struggling students with a calculator. Everyone agreed after careful analysis of student processes that direct instruction in problem solving would prove more beneficial.

In addition to the universal Tier 1 differentiated instruction, the team decided to ask the math coach or the university tutors to work with the five students three times a week for 20 minutes each time. One of the team members reminded Mr. Gibbs that the university tutors and math coach would no longer be available to the ninth-grade team after the end of the month. He indicated that he can carve time to assist the students during the independent activity time during his math schedule at least three times a week. Students were provided with step-by-step processes and exploratory problem-solving opportunities. Exhibit 2.4 describes some of the intervention strategies that the team discussed during their meeting.

 IMPLEMENTATION TIP

The Math team discussed a variety of options based on their assessment shown in Exhibit 2.4. Here are additional items they discussed to help them decide on the implementation:

► **IInterventions** may include time, such as duration and frequency (e.g., 20, 30, 45 minutes a day, two times a week, daily); environment (physical location, structure); personnel (teacher, specialist); and grouping (small 1:5 or 1:3, heterogeneous, homogenous). The higher the tier, the smaller the group and the formative assessment (two times a month, weekly, two times a week, daily). The higher the tier, the more frequent the need for assessment to monitor the student's progress. Remember, core Tier 1 provides the research-based instruction with differentiation as needed, based on the pre-assessed needs of the students from a highly qualified teacher during core instruction. Students in Tiers 2–3 require intensified intervention strategies and activities.

► **Strategies** shown are samples of the intentional adult actions that should have the greatest positive impact on student learning, such as the use of advance organizers and explicit direct instruction. Select the strategy based on the strengths, challenges, and inferences discussed during the meeting.

► **Activities** shown are the actions of the student, such as highlighting key math vocabulary post-it notes as cue and note reminders.

NOTE: This is not intended to be an exhaustive list of possible activities and strategies for this area of content. Typically, there is not a dividing line between some of the tiers. It may be that the strategy or classroom activity will be appropriate for multiple tiers. In some cases, the time, intensity, and duration of a strategy may be modified to suit particular groups or individual students. Read the "How Does It Look" section to see which strategy, activity, and assessment was used by this particular team. Discuss other strategies that may be appropriate based on the scenario.

 HOW DOES IT LOOK?

At the beginning of the math lesson, Mr. Gibbs asked the students (as usual) to do a small bell-ringer activity. He asked five students to join him and distributed an advance organizer that would help them follow the steps to solve the word problems that he would be presenting to the rest of the class. The students in Tier 2 and Tier 3 would participate in the same direct instruction (Tier 1) lesson with their peers but additionally they would have the advance organizer to help structure their steps on paper.

EXHIBIT 2.4   **Sample Mathematics Skills***

Sample Tiers	Strategies and Activities	Description
2, 3	Math coach or university volunteer tutor 20 minutes 2–3 times a week	A math coach, tutor, retired teacher or other interventionist can push-in or pull-out a small group of students in Tier 2. Push-in can be accomplished with learning stations or during cooperative learning groups.
2, 3	Advance organizers	Students are provided with an organizer in advance of the lesson that explicitly highlights the problem-solving steps.
1, 2, 3	Math strategies notebook	Provide explicit instruction on this graphic organizer. Students are to write each new mathematics problem on the left side and fill in how it was solved on the right side of the graphic.
2, 3	Highlighted vocabulary	Vocabulary should be translated into the numerals or operations to be used for each section.
1, 2, 3	Step-by-step word problems	The teacher can provide in writing and through modeling and demonstrating in small sections a step-by-step process to solve problems. Remember to provide opportunity for inquiry.
2, 3	Additional practice time	Students in Tiers 2 and 3 are provided with additional time during class, (e.g., during flex activities, warm-up, or independent practice).
2, 3	Tutorial	Targeted tutoring provided before, during, or after school. Interventionist can supplement not supplant instruction 15–30 minutes, 1–5 times per week.
Additional:		
Additional:		
Additional:		

* Note: This is not meant as an exhaustive list of the instructional strategies, interventions, or activities.

Sources: Ainsworth and Christinson, 2006; Stein, Silbert, and Carnine, 1997; House, 2004.

Mr. Gibbs's discussion with these students took about three to four minutes. He told them to follow along with the class, and as everyone began their guided practice, he saw how they were doing and answered additional questions. Mr. Gibbs knew it was crucial to make sure the students understood that he would check on them and not allow them to feel lost or become frustrated. In the past, he had noticed that students tended to misbehave or actually stop trying to figure things out if they felt they would not receive additional help. Mr. Gibbs also found that providing alternative instruction to mixed groups of students allowed the students to know that they would all receive individual or small-group attention at some point during the week. This was a helpful way for him to manage the time and for students not to feel embarrassed or singled out. Students would be able to see rapid improvement in their problem solving if they continued using the graphic organizers that outlined the step-by-step process.

In addition to using the advance organizers and highlighted vocabulary, Mr. Gibbs spoke to both the university tutor and the instructional coach for math. The coach suggested using university tutors because they have excellent rapport, especially with the ninth graders at the school. Mr. Gibbs decided to provide three options for a push-in: (1) a university tutor would come into the class, (2) a comfortable alcove would be arranged for tutors, or (3) students could come before or after school. All five of the students opted for the alcove; they said they could concentrate better. To manage the time, Mr. Gibbs arranged for the tutors to work with the students during the independent practice segment of his class. He also asked for a reconsideration of extra time with the tutors before or after school. But he promised the students he would first wait to see how they responded to the extra small-group (homogenous) intervention. Mr. Gibbs felt confident that after the tutors left he would be able to continue working with small groups of students during class sessions to support their learning as the other students worked on independent assignments.

> **Reflection:** *Jennifer is beginning to express embarrassment at the need to use advance organizers and strategies notebooks in the ninth grade. Can you suggest additional age-appropriate strategies that might suit her needs?*

 ## HOW IS IT MONITORED?

The ninth-grade math department team suggested that for the Tier 2 students a short math formative assessment be given on average once or twice a week immediately following the exercises. Frequently, all of the math activities culminate with an end-of-unit assessment for the whole class, but Mr. Gibbs indicated that he could be flexible and provide the assessments to the targeted students as part of their bell-ringer activity or as an entrance slip once or twice per week. The team also suggested that those students in Tier 3 take a very short assessment three to four times per week. This would be a quick method to see if adjustments needed to take place to help the students during class. Next, Mr. Gibbs and his ninth-grade math team gave a sheet of preprinted graph paper to all students in Tier 2 and Tier 3 and asked them to keep track of their own scores in each area assessed. He knew that with over 150 students a day he would need to enlist the aid of his targeted students in the progress-monitoring process. He told the students that these scores would help them see their progress and provide topics to be discussed with them to help move ahead. The students were quickly shown how to chart their own scores, and after a little practice they started to learn how to analyze their own performance issues. Mr. Gibbs reported to the team that the individual student and peer analysis was an unexpected outcome of the process. After the scores were charted, he took a few minutes to discuss the progress of each student and what they would do next. The ninth-grade teachers indicated that the students responded in a very mature manner regarding their needs. They actually started volunteering suggestions to help them achieve their goals for each new section of learning. In one of his classes, Mr. Gibbs experimented with an interactive notebook in which students wrote their comments and feelings about the work. It was designed like a hard copy blog. At times he would write his comments, and that worked well. He told the content department team that with over 150 students it was not possible to respond to every journal on a daily basis, so he selected those to read and respond to based on certain concerns he had for each student at different times. It simply gave him another method of communicating with students if he could not personally speak with them within the week. He also based his decisions of how to communicate with the students on the learning style of each student. For example, some students needed to hear the information from him face-to-face, while others could comprehend and communicate well through the interactive notebook. He was careful to make sure that students dated all of their work samples and assessments, and he took the results every two weeks to his colleagues on the team for additional feedback. Students who were responding well to the intervention strategies continued until they could work independently with proficient scores in Tier 1. Those students who continued to need targeted attention were flagged for additional analysis. The team looked for a variety of issues that might be impacting the students including setting, curriculum, technology, timing, frequency, duration, intensity, program, methodology, personnel—any areas of intervention that perhaps needed adjustment for the next two-week period. These decisions were documented on the progress monitoring form.

HOW HAVE YOU THOUGHT ABOUT?

Students of all grade levels often struggle with math computation and word problems. Mathematical reasoning and number sense are just as important as being able to read. Math illiteracy can seriously handicap students in school and adults in later life. Successful intervention is dependent on finding the cause of the math deficiency. As teachers question "What causes math problems?" three areas should be considered that impact math learning: (1) foundational skills (problem solving), (2) mathematical skills (computation and counting), and (3) math vocabulary and symbols.

As you reflect on the three students in Tier 2, think about how their situation applies to your teaching and learning. Consider these questions:

► How can the use of manipulatives and kinesthetic learning activities help students improve math skills?

► How can math journals help students improve their math skills?

► What vocabulary strategies can you use to help students comprehend the complex terminology used in math problems?

CHAPTER THREE

Tier 3 Scenarios

TIER 3 SNAPSHOT

What: Tier 3 instructional intervention is high-quality, research-based, core instruction, targeted and intensive.

Who: Tier 3 instructional intervention may be provided by a highly qualified licensed professional, such as a general education teacher, instructional coach, or a certified/licensed specialist.

Where: Instruction in Tier 3 typically takes place in the general-education classroom, lab, or a learning resource center.

When: Intensity of the time, duration and frequency of the instructional intervention, and progress monitoring may be increased as determined by the grade level or content discipline team based on the pre-assessed needs of the student.

Why: Approximately 1 to 5 percent of the students who do not respond as expected to core Tier 1 and Tier 2 instructional interventions may require intensive small group or individual assistance.

Steven
Primary

(Phonemic Awareness)

Steven is a very active five-year-old student. He is the youngest of five siblings who are all much older and from a previous marriage. His older siblings like to play with Steven, but only one 16-year-old brother, Jared, is still living at home. Steven loves to play. But he throws massive temper tantrums at school when he does not get his way. When describing his behavior to her fellow kindergarten teachers, Ms. Cherish was told she should express the words "temper tantrum" in observable terms. So she described his tantrums as screaming for 10 to 30 minutes at a time and biting and kicking when he does not get his way or is told to do something he does not like to do. His favorite word is "No!" Ms. Cherish carefully documents and reports Steven's behavior to his parents several times a week. During the last parent-teacher conference night, his parents indicated that Steven exhibits exactly the same behaviors at home. Both parents feel that he is catered to by his visiting siblings and has learned negative behaviors. His mother said she just doesn't know what to do. Ms. Cherish's more immediate concern is Steven's lack of progress with lessons in phonemic awareness. She feels strongly that his behaviors are interfering with his academic progress. His universal screening indicated that he is doing well in math concepts but does not focus long enough without a behavior outburst to learn to read at the same rate as his classmates.

During a recent grade-level team meeting of kindergarten teachers, Ms. Cherish was asked to describe how Steven attempts to process phonemic awareness. They wanted to know specifically what he can do (strengths) and the areas that he is struggling with (challenges). She was also asked to make a few inferences so they could consider a possible root cause. The first comment that Ms. Cherish made was that she felt he had so many behavioral issues that he did not focus on the sounds at all. A team member asked if she had checked his files for sensory or health issues. Ms. Cherish said of course that was her first action; Steven does not have any vision or hearing issues. She said he and two other students in class simply glance at the words and quickly become distracted by some other activity. Another teacher with very strong reading scores for her kindergarten class suggested that they try using the kinesthetic, verbal, and tactile activities of the students to their advantage. The team decided to follow the research provided by the National Institute for Literacy to help with the Tier 3 intensive intervention for Steven and a few other students who were struggling with phonemic awareness.

Ms. Cherish decided to target the students who were significantly below proficiency in phonemic awareness to help them begin to notice, think about, and work with (manipulate) sounds in spoken language. They would spend the next two weeks using a variety of activities to build phonemic awareness by adding more physical and tactile activities that would engage them and help them gain the content and skill required for the next two weeks. It was decided that an additional 15 minutes daily would help target skills for Steven and a few of his classmates. Ms. Cherish began to work with them three to five minutes at a time with the goal of 15 minutes. They began with phoneme isolation. To help the students focus and diminish behavioral outbursts, the activities were presented as physical and tactile as well as visual and auditory. There were times when the activity involved shouting out, writing in clay, hopping, clapping, using their bodies as shapes, and running from one spot in the room to another. The key was repetition but in a variety of active ways that caught the students' attention. Ms. Cherish felt that she could provide this additional time when the other students were actively involved in a choice or preferred activity. Three parents also volunteered to have their children either come 15 to 20 minutes early three times a week or stay after school 15 to 20 minutes to be tutored. The parents, including Steven's mother, would bring their children and watch during the lesson so some of the activities could be carried out at home. This really surprised Ms. Cherish, but she was delighted. She realized that not every parent has that flexibility in their day; some must hold down two-and-a-half jobs to make ends meet. But she was grateful for the extra support. The parents were shown specific strategies that could help students at home so that the lessons were reinforced at home and at school. Exhibit 3.1 lists the additional intervention strategies that would be used for the students throughout the semester. Before beginning their plan, the teachers were reminded that they should check the vision and hearing records of the students as well.

> **Reflection:** *Steven is described as a very active oppositional student. How would you address his behaviors within the context of using the strategies shown below for phonemic awareness?*

IMPLEMENTATION TIP

The grade-level team discussed a variety of options based on their assessment shown in Exhibit 3.1. Here are additional items they discussed to help them decide on the implementation:

► **Interventions** may include time, such as duration and frequency (e.g., 20, 30, 45 minutes a day, two times a week, daily); environment (physical location, structure); personnel (teacher, specialist); and grouping (small 1:5 or 1:3, heterogeneous, homogenous). The higher the tier, the smaller the group and the formative assessment (two times a month, weekly, two times a week, daily). The higher the tier, the more frequent the need for assessment to monitor the student's progress. Remember, core Tier 1 provides the research-based instruction with differentiation as needed, based on the pre-assessed needs of the students from a highly qualified teacher during core instruction. Students in Tiers 2–3 require intensified intervention strategies and activities.

► **Strategies** shown are samples of the intentional adult actions that should have the greatest positive impact on student learning, such as the the direct instruction of phonemic additions. Select the strategy based on the strengths, challenges, and inferences discussed during the meeting.

► **Activities** shown are the actions of the student, such as making a new word by adding a phoneme to an existing word.

NOTE: This is not intended to be an exhaustive list of possible activities and strategies for this area of content. Typically, there is not a dividing line between some of the tiers. It may be that the strategy or classroom activity will be appropriate for multiple tiers. In some cases, the time, intensity, and duration of a strategy may be modified to suit particular groups or individual students. Read the "How Does It Look" section to see which strategy, activity, and assessment was used by this particular team. Discuss other strategies that may be appropriate based on the scenario.

 HOW DOES IT LOOK?

The teachers of the kindergarten program decided to begin their new intervention plan for phonemic awareness the next school day (Monday). They conducted a short pre-assessment to determine exactly which component of phonemic awareness each of the four to five students in each of their classes was continuing to struggle with. Next, they provided direct instruction, either 1:1 or 1:5, five times per week with the intensive students while other students either worked on independent practice, computer programs, flex choice, or at learning centers. Three of the students in Ms. Cherish's class came for tutorial before school with their parents, and two students with specific learning disabilities received Specially Designed Instruction (SDI) required by their Individualized Education Program (IEP) on a push-in basis three times a week from the special education teacher. Ms. Cherish felt that trying these interventions along with the behavior interventions of the Positive

EXHIBIT 3.1 **Sample Phonemic Awareness***

Sample Tiers	Strategies and Activities	Description
2, 3	Phoneme isolation	Students recognize individual sounds in a word. The teachers may use a variety of kinesthetic, tactile, auditory, and visual methods. These strategies were used successfully in each of the items shown in the remaining cells of this chart.
1, 2, 3	Phoneme identity	Students recognize the same sounds in different words.
1, 2, 3	Phoneme categorization	Students recognize the word in a set of three or four words that have the "odd" sound.
1, 2, 3	Phoneme blending	Students listen to a sequence of separately spoken phonemes and then combine the phonemes to form a word. Then they write and read the word.
1, 2, 3	Phoneme segmentation	Students break a word into its separate sounds, saying each sound as they tap out or count it. Then they write and read the word.
1, 2, 3	Phoneme deletion	Students recognize the word that remains when a phoneme is removed from another word.
1, 2, 3	Phoneme addition	Students make a new word by adding a phoneme to an existing word.
1, 2, 3	Phoneme substitution	Students substitute one phoneme for another to make a new word.
2, 3	Additional guided practice	Students were given an additional 15 minutes a day. The work time began with 3 to 5 minutes building to 15 minutes. The teacher kept note of their time on graph paper with a check mark next to minute increments.
2, 3	Tutorial	Students received supplemental assistance 15 to 20 minutes three times per week with either the classroom teacher or an interventionist. This was before, during (flex), or after school. During school is at the discretion of the team but should not supplant direct core instruction.
3	Special education	Special education teacher worked directly with the students who required intensive intervention. Three of the 5 students had an Individualized Education Program (IEP) in reading. Specially Designed Instruction (SDI)** was used to assist students.
Additional:		
Additional:		
Additional:		

* Note: This is not meant as an exhaustive list of the instructional strategies, interventions, or activities.
** Specially Designed Instruction (SDI) takes into account the content skills, student strengths, and challenges as well as the disability in order to design instruction to meet the needs of individual students.

Source: Literacy and Information Communication System (LINCS) http://lincs.ed.gov

Behavioral Instructional Support (PBIS) program should make a significant difference for Steven and his classmates who were receiving the intensive Tier 3 support. This same structure was used in each of the kindergarten classes for students requiring Tier 3 intensive intervention.

 HOW IS IT MONITORED?

In order to confirm that students were responding appropriately to the selected scientifically research-based interventions, the grade-level team of kindergarten teachers decided to chart the progress of students on two strategies listed in Exhibit 3.1. They decided that 80 percent accuracy would be their target. They also decided to provide common formative assessments in each area on a weekly basis and to report to their team on a bimonthly basis. Periodically throughout the semester the team of kindergarten teachers also invited other staff members to help them strategize additional activities that could support their reading plans. For example, they invited the speech and language pathologist (SLP), occupational therapist (OT), physical therapist (PT), art and music teachers as well as the counselor and social worker to the meeting for their suggestions and feedback. They would also work closely with the special education teacher to help them incorporate differentiated instructional strategies into their general (Tier 1 and Tier 2) instruction with the students.

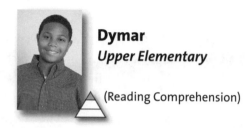

Dymar
Upper Elementary

(Reading Comprehension)

Dymar is one of the most popular students in school. He is friendly, outgoing, helpful, thoughtful, and cooperative. He tries very hard to comply with the instructions of his teacher. He loves art, listening to music, playing all types of computer games, talking to his friends, and playing sports. Due to slow academic performance, Dymar was retained in the first grade. At this point, he is basically a year older than his classmates. His mother feels it was not a good decision. She worries that he is now even further behind. Dymar is still significantly behind grade level, but he demonstrates confidence and a maturity that has opened him to really trying hard to succeed in school.

Based on Dymar's test scores and multiple unsuccessful responses to Tier 1 and Tier 2 interventions, the grade-level team decided to send Dymar's records to the Student Teacher Assistance Team (STAT). The team discussed the results of the well-documented interventions that were tried after his retention and expressed concern that Dymar was not responding appropriately to core instruction at Tier 1 or Tier 2 instructional interventions. The gap was continuing, and the team felt that he required assessment for special education. Dymar's mother indicated that she was pleased with everything the school had tried to do to help her son and agreed that perhaps he might need more intensive intervention including the possible services of a special educator to help him. She also felt Dymar had a very good relationship with his teacher and was indeed doing his best. She consented to the battery of assessments for eligibility. In Dymar's home state, both response to scientifically research-based intervention and a discrepancy model are required for qualification as a student with a Specific Learning Disability (SLD).

During the interdisciplinary meeting for the IEP, it was determined that Dymar indeed met the qualifications as a student with an SLD, specifically in the area of reading comprehension. The team carefully reviewed his present levels of performance and documented responses to Tier 1 and Tier 2 interventions. They also documented results from a battery of assessments conducted by the school's diagnostician. His highly qualified fourth-grade general education teacher, Mr. Chiang, as well as the IEP team were confident that Dymar's current and previous teachers had done an excellent job of providing positive intervention strategies, progress monitoring, and charting of Dymar's responses at each interval. The reading curriculum adopted by the district was also completely aligned with the state standards and closely aligned with the mandated state assessments. The grade-level team knew that the gap, especially in reading comprehension, would continue to widen if they didn't begin intensive interventions for Dymar with the assistance of SDI from the special education teacher. Dymar's scores in mathematics are at the 2.5 grade level. Exhibit 3.2 provides some of the scientifically research-based intervention strategies that Mr. Chiang used as a result of the team's analysis of Dymar's current strengths and challenges and the team's inferences regarding his reading comprehension.

> **Reflection:** *The grade-level team has indicated that Dymar requires an additional 45 minutes daily of reading instruction. If he was a student in your classroom, how could you address this requirement?*

IMPLEMENTATION TIP

The grade-level team discussed a variety of options based on their assessment shown in Exhibit 3.2. Here are additional items they discussed to help them decide on the implementation:

▶ **Interventions** may include time, such as duration and frequency (e.g., 20, 30, 45 minutes a day, two times a week, daily); environment (physical location, structure); personnel (teacher, specialist); and grouping (small 1:5 or 1:3, heterogeneous, homogenous). The higher the tier, the smaller the group and the formative assessment (two times a month, weekly, two times a week, daily). The higher the tier, the more frequent the need for assessment to monitor the student's progress. Remember, core Tier 1 provides the research-based instruction with differentiation as needed, based on the pre-assessed needs of the students from a highly qualified teacher during core instruction. Students in Tiers 2–3 require intensified intervention strategies and activities.

EXHIBIT 3.2 **Sample Text Comprehension**

Sample Tiers	Strategies and Activities	Description
2, 3	Extended time 45 minutes after school	Attend an after-school program to supplement core and targeted instruction in reading comprehension 2–3 times per week.
2, 3	Alternate instruction	Provide visual cues or mini-lesson in advance of core instruction.
2, 3	Monitoring comprehension	Identify where the difficulty occurs, identify what the difficulty is, restate the difficult sentence or passage in their own words. Look back through the text, look forward in the text for information that might help them to resolve the difficulty.
2, 3	Metacognition skill development	Learn to use metacognitive strategies to think about and have control over reading.
2, 3	Graphic and semantic organizers	Use graphic organizers (e.g., maps, webs, graphs, charts, frames, or clusters) to focus on concepts and how they are related to other concepts. These tools visually represent information and help with organization.
2, 3	Answering questions	Students learn to answer questions that require an understanding of information that is: • text explicit (stated explicitly in a single sentence), • text implicit (implied by information presented in two or more sentences), or • information not found in the text at all but part of the reader's prior knowledge or experience.
2, 3	Generating questions	Students were taught to ask themselves questions that require them to integrate information from different segments of text. For example, students can be taught to ask main-idea questions that relate to important information in a text.
2, 3	Recognizing story structure	Students learn to identify the categories of content (setting, initiating events, internal reactions, goals, attempts, and outcomes) and how this content is organized into a plot. Graphic organizers such as story maps were used to show the sequence of events and organization.
2, 3	Summarizing	Identify or generate main ideas, connect the main or central ideas, eliminate redundant and unnecessary information, and remember what they read.
	Special education	Participate in Specially Designed Instruction (SDI) from the special education teacher.
2, 3	Prior knowledge	As part of previewing, ask students what they already know about the content of the selection. Ask them what they know about the author and what text structure is likely to be used. Discuss the important vocabulary used in the text. Show students some pictures or diagrams to prepare them for what they are about to read.
2, 3	Mental imagery	Help readers form mental pictures, or images, as they read. Make sure the vocabulary is clear and if necessary provide visual images so the students have a frame of reference for the mental imagery. (Google Images is a quick resource for finding pictures.)
Additional:		
Additional:		
Additional:		

Sources: Literacy and Information Communication System (LINCS) http://lincs.ed.gov
Marzano, 2001; Pierangelo, 2003.

► **Strategies** shown are samples of the intentional adult actions that should have the greatest positive impact on student learning, such as the use of graphic and semantic organizers. Select the strategy based on the strengths, challenges, and inferences discussed during the meeting.

► **Activities** shown are the actions of the student, such as generating questions.

NOTE: This is not intended to be an exhaustive list of possible activities and strategies for this area of content. Typically, there is not a dividing line between some of the tiers. It may be that the strategy or classroom activity will be appropriate for multiple tiers. In some cases, the time, intensity, and duration of a strategy may be modified to suit particular groups or individual students. Read the "How Does It Look" section to see which strategy, activity, and assessment was used by this particular team. Discuss other strategies that may be appropriate based on the scenario.

 ## HOW DOES IT LOOK?

Dymar showed favorable responses to only a few of the text comprehension intervention strategies that Mr. Chiang tried immediately following the IEP meeting. The special education teacher provided a copy of the goals and objectives. Mr. Chiang participated in the meeting and was pleased to see that the focus was helping Dymar meet grade-level proficiency in the state reading standards for the fourth grade. Specifically, Dymar and a few of his other classmates in Tier 3 were taught story structures used in a variety of genre, were provided with semantic organizers, and were taught how to use mental imagery. Dymar met with the special education teacher on a push-in basis to supplement his instruction with SDI to address the specific learning disability 2 times, 30 minutes each per week. Mr. Chiang collected data that documented the interventions for Dymar and his classmates in Tier 3.

 ## HOW IS IT MONITORED?

Mr. Chiang was asked to continue his documentation of classroom intervention strategies and to team-teach in reading with the special education teacher. The IEP team designated 30 minutes twice a week for SDI that would be provided by the special educator and Mr. Chiang. Both teachers shared the responsibility of monitoring Dymar's progress and sharing the information with the fourth-grade team on a bimonthly basis as well as at the annual IEP meeting. The goal was to work toward moving Dymar from intensive level support, back to targeted support, and then to universal instruction. The school psychologist reminded the team that the interventions must be intense enough to make at least two years' progress each year in order to close this significant gap. To accomplish this, during each informal assessment (three times a week), the general and special education teachers discussed the appropriateness of the level in terms of strategy, time, duration, and intensity. Adjustments were documented between each grade-level meeting.

Mario
Secondary

(Writing)

Mario enrolled in his current district six weeks after the beginning of school. He is shy, but has been described as a good listener, soft spoken, and charming. So far, his favorite subjects include music and mathematics. The result of his universal assessment showed that his academics were significantly delayed in writing. Initially, his ninth-grade teachers were concerned that there may have been a second issue with language. According to his Home Language Survey, both of his parents speak English at home, were born in Albuquerque, New Mexico, and speak, read, and write fluently in English. Mario is a third-generation student born in America. He is also fluent in Spanish, as he visits his grandparents frequently in Chihuahua, Mexico, and he began taking Spanish classes as an eighth-grader at his previous school in Phoenix. Although Mario has a difficult time with writing, he does not seem to have problems expressing himself verbally. When interviewed by his English composition teacher, Mr. Pederson, Mario indicated that he knows what he wants to write but just has problems organizing his thoughts to put them on paper appropriately. He also struggles in science and social studies, but his lowest scores consistently appear to be in writing.

Mr. Pederson said that Mario is a delight to have in class, but he is concerned that after trying all of the Tier 1 and Tier 2 writing interventions, Mario has not responded as expected. Mr. Pederson indicated that Mario studies hard and has expressed embarrassment regarding his writing skills. In the few weeks that he has attended school, he has watched with disappointment as his grades in core content classes have plummeted. Mario confided in a friend that he is so discouraged with school that he is thinking of dropping out and trying to get a job with his uncle, the owner of a building construction business in Phoenix.

After collecting data from the universal assessments and bimonthly common formative assessments, the content-area team indicated that they would need to continue to analyze the data to make intensive intervention recommendations for Mario. Mr. Pederson contacted Mario's previous school in Phoenix to see if he had an IEP and discovered that he had not qualified three months ago. But they did indicate that last school year Mario had been involved in a severe auto accident that required extensive medical treatment and individual tutors for his core classes. For several months he was unable to write, but dictation was allowed by the school to help him demonstrate knowledge of the course content. The tutor who provided hospital and then homebound instruction for Mario said that Mario made remarkable progress considering his physical condition at the time. Mr. Pederson shared this information with his team members and stated that Mario was doing well in most classes, but his scores were still depressed due to his poor writing skills. The team felt that after reviewing data from all of Mario's informal assessments they would be able to analyze his current performance issues more accurately. Mr. Pederson suggested that Mario be referred to the STAT for consideration for special education again. Ms. Smythe, a fellow ninth-grade English teacher on the English department team, suggested that they not jump to the conclusion that he needs a referral for special education just yet. She pointed out that according to Mr. Pederson's report, Mario had suffered major trauma. He lost a twin brother in the auto accident and spent many hours away from classroom instruction during his convalescence. After carefully analyzing Mario's work samples, Ms. Smythe and the rest of the team members felt strongly that specific intervention strategies should be provided first along with close progress monitoring to see exactly how Mario responded before making a referral. The school has a strong group of core instructors in English, social studies, mathematics, and science. Ms. Smythe assured Mr. Pederson that he would not be alone in his attempts to assist Mario. In fact, the other teachers agreed that there were other students on campus in the ninth grade who fit a similar profile of struggling in their writing skills. They felt that a multidisciplinary team could be formed to pinpoint those few students in each class that could benefit from the strategies that they would use for Mario. They would take an "all hands on deck" approach to help students in this Tier 3 level of instruction. Some of the students are general education, some are special education, and some are ELLs.

The multidisciplinary team meeting was held the next afternoon with a team leader representative from each of the core content departments. The writing problems discussed in the initial English department team meeting were described. The other team leaders for content agreed that they were experiencing the same problem. One person confessed that he felt it was the English department's dilemma and that his only concern should be specific course content. But he really liked this concept of a team approach so that the students could receive similar direction throughout the day, and the teachers could receive support from each other as well. Exhibit 3.3 provides a list of some of the interventions previously tried by the English teachers for students in Tier 1 and Tier 2, as well as interventions for students in Tier 3.

> **Reflection:** *What additional information do you believe is important to know about Mario's physical condition following the auto accident before beginning any of the intervention strategies shown below? Would you suggest an alternative intervention based on the information provided in the scenario?*

IMPLEMENTATION TIP

The English Department Team team discussed a variety of options based on their assessment shown in Exhibit 3.3. Here are additional items they discussed to help them decide on the implementation:

▶ **Interventions** may include time, such as duration and frequency (e.g., 20, 30, 45 minutes a day, two times a week, daily); environment (physical location, structure); personnel (teacher, specialist); and grouping (small 1:5 or 1:3, heterogeneous, homogenous). The higher the tier, the smaller the group and the formative assessment (two times a month, weekly, two times a week, daily). The higher the tier, the more frequent the need for assessment to monitor the student's progress. Remember, core Tier 1 provides the research-based instruction with differentiation as needed, based on the pre-assessed needs of the students from a highly qualified teacher during core instruction. Students in Tiers 2–3 require intensified intervention strategies and activities.

▶ **Strategies** shown in the chart below are samples of the intentional adult actions that should have the greatest positive impact on student learning, such as the use of alternative instruction, advance organizers, and nonlinguistic representations. Select the strategy based on the strengths, challenges, and inferences discussed during the meeting.

▶ **Activities** shown in the chart below are the actions of the teacher. The actions of the student may be keeping a daily content vocabulary log.

NOTE: This is not intended to be an exhaustive list of possible activities and strategies for this area of content. Typically, there is not a dividing line between some of the tiers. It may be that the strategy or classroom activity will be appro-

EXHIBIT 3.3 **Sample Writing**

Sample Tiers	Strategies and Activities	Description
2, 3	Extended time (45 minutes) after school	Students were offered additional time twice each week for supplemental writing practice under the guidance of one of the English teachers. (Teachers rotated their time as an interventionist with small groups of students.)
2, 3	Advance organizers	Writing organizers were demonstrated and formats provided to students to help with organization of writing.
2, 3	Alternate instruction	Students were provided with rubrics and exemplars in advance of the writing lesson.
2, 3	In-school tutorial 30 minutes, three times a week	Students who received supplemental services in Tier 3 met with a member of the Core of Retired Teachers and university student volunteers to help supplement the core instruction of the general education teacher. This was conducted on scheduled flex-activity assignment days or during prearranged cooperative learning sections of class. Records were kept and monitored by each student's teacher or interventionist.
1, 2, 3	Entrance/Exit slips	Students were provided with either an entrance or an exit slip assessment (short 1–3 questions or prompts) daily. To save scoring time, students may quickly learn to score and chart many of their own slips.
3	Special education services two times a week for 45 minutes	Specially Designed Instruction provided for those students eligible for special education services.
	Parallel teaching	Classes may be split in half with two teachers using the same content but in some cases using different processes or methods to help students with the lesson. This may be done to lower the overall class size of instruction or to create smaller, homogeneous groups of students for the lesson, as needed.
	Team teaching	Both the general and special education teachers work together to provide writing lessons for all three tiers to address the needs of individual students.
Additional:		
Additional:		
Additional:		

Sources: Peery, 2010;
   Literacy and Information Communication System (LINCS) http://lincs.ed.gov
   U.S. Department of Education, Institute of Education Sciences, What Works Clearinghouse at http://ies.ed.gov/ncee/wwc/

priate for multiple tiers. In some cases, the time, intensity, and duration of a strategy may be modified to suit particular groups or individual students. Read the "How Does It Look" section to see which strategy, activity, and assessment was used by this particular team. Discuss other strategies that may be appropriate based on the scenario.

HOW DOES IT LOOK?

The core teachers use a series of co-teaching strategies whenever possible to help Mario and a few other students in Tier 3 with their writing skills. The teachers use a combination of preplanned interventions throughout the 60 minutes of instruction. The introduction and direct instruction portions of the lesson are given by either the general education teacher or the interventionist. The intervention strategies agreed to by the department team members included extended time (45 minutes after school) with one of the English teachers in a small-group setting and alternative instruction that included rubrics and exemplars in advance of the writing lessons. Additionally, whenever possible, the teachers plan together and decide which co-teaching model to use with which students and when it would take place. Mario indicated that he wanted to continue with the after-school program as well; he was benefiting from the small-group instruction. He said that the individual attention was helping him close the achievement gap, and he started noticing his grades improve in all of his classes.

HOW IS IT MONITORED?

The multidisciplinary team meeting was held with team leaders on a bimonthly basis. One of the special education teachers was asked if she could make time to lend her expertise to the meeting as well. This teacher was split between so many classes she didn't understand how it would be possible. She said she would determine her attendance based on the severity of the students' needs, the largest number of students with IEPs, or by specific request for consultation with her general education colleagues. Ms. Henry indicated that it would be a lot easier for her to help her colleagues in a multidisciplinary meeting rather than by individual departments; she would be able to attend more frequently. The team leaders volunteered to be responsible for monitoring the progress of their own departments and to bring the analyzed data to the multidisciplinary team meeting to help determine adjustments that might be required for the interventions.

 HOW HAVE YOU THOUGHT ABOUT?

Students in Tier 3 intervention require individualized, intensive, and strategic interventions that target the students' skill deficits. These students have not achieved the desired results in Tier 1 (differentiated instruction) or Tier 2 (targeted intervention). They are referred for comprehensive evaluations and considered for additional education services under the Individuals with Disabilities Education Improvement Act of 2004 (IDEIA, 2004). Teachers should provide intensive, systematic instruction in the skill area(s) needed in reading, writing, and math for those who score below the benchmark on universal screenings.

As you reflect on the three students in Tier 3, think about how their situation applies to your teaching and learning. Consider these questions:

► How do you differentiate for students needing extra support with learning?

► What type of collaborative planning do you have with special education support teachers? How do you communicate successes and challenges observed in your students?

► How can visual representations be used to help students with comprehension, vocabulary acquisition, and understanding new content?

► How can pre-assessments be used to guide a teacher's new instruction to students?

CHAPTER FOUR

Special Education Scenarios

 SPECIAL EDUCATION SNAPSHOT

What: Students with an Individualized Education Plan (IEP) will receive Tier 1 core instruction along with their peers from the highly qualified, general-education teacher. Accommodation, modification, and differentiation is used for students based on their pre-assessed need. Students will also receive additional Specially Designed Instruction (SDI) from the special education teacher in the general-education class (push-in model) or in a lab or resource learning center (pull-out model) as designated by the area of need listed on the IEP. Secondary students may be assigned to an additional class for targeted or intensive instruction.

Who: Tier 2 instructional intervention may be provided by a highly qualified general-education teacher or qualified specialist (e.g., reading or math coach or licensed special education teacher). The determination of who may provide the direct service is a district decision. Specific minutes of SDI listed on the IEP is provided by the special education teacher.

Where: Instruction in Tiers 1, 2, and 3 typically takes place in a collaborative general-education classroom. In a few cases however, students are pulled out for specific training as needed by a designed specialist during Tiers 2 and 3.

When: Intensity of the time, duration and frequency of the targeted or intensive instructional intervention, and progress monitoring may be determined by the IEP Team members based on the pre-assessed needs of the student. The core instruction of Tier 1 should not be supplanted. In this case, the goal is to ensure access to the general education curriculum.

Why: Students in special education may receive a variety of services based on present levels of performance in one or more areas. The special education teacher is licensed to provide SDI based on the IEP. For areas not defined by the IEP, the goals and objectives for instruction would be the same as those listed by the student's peers in Tiers 1 or 2.

Karen
Primary

(Sequencing information)

Karen is a very active kindergarten student. Prior to enrolling in kindergarten, Karen's mother was concerned that Karen was having difficulty with gross and fine motor skills. She also noticed that Karen had slight speech articulation issues and problems following simple one-step directions. She took Karen at the age of three years old to a screening for a program called Child Find. Through this public school program Karen received special services in her school beginning at age three. When Karen began kindergarten it was determined by the multidisciplinary team that Karen would be listed as a noncategorical student and continue to receive special services that began in the program for three- and four-year-olds.

During the regular bimonthly meeting of the kindergarten grade-level team, Karen's kindergarten teacher, Mr. Stein, explained that based on the data collected over the last two weeks, Karen was making great progress in her fine and gross motor skills. The speech and language pathologist indicated that Karen may still require speech therapy for a longer period of time, at least through the school year. Mr. Stein's greatest concern at this point is that Karen continues to have difficulty following directions and reciting information in sequence as presented. He believes this will hinder her academic progress. Karen is a very polite, cooperative student who is eager to participate in all classroom activities. She appears to try very hard to follow the teacher's directions but without success.

The instructional coach asked Mr. Stein to explain in more detail exactly what Karen's difficulty is in following directions. Mr. Stein indicated that Karen appears to listen but not understand the direction given; for example, when asked to repeat numbers or letters, either individually or with her classmates, she struggles to continue past the first two or three letters. Mr. Stein shared with the team that he did look at Karen's records to make sure that her hearing screening had been done and found that Karen does have normal hearing. He also looked at the three- and four-year-old program records for Karen and noted that the classroom teacher indicated the same problem for Karen: not being able to continue in sequence past a certain number. Mr. Stein also noticed that Karen had difficulty sequencing three objects or following more than one direction at a time.

The team members for kindergarten suggested a series of pre-assessment for Karen as well as for a few other students in the kindergarten program. The assessment included one-, two-, and three-step directions and a series of short sequences of from one to five items. Some of the sequence items were on paper, some items were photographs of objects or short sections from a story, and some were tangible manipulative items. The team determined that Karen could recognize numbers, letters, and parts of stories, but her challenge was the ability to see them in sequence or put them together as a whole. Karen's teacher noticed that she appears to learn best through tactile and kinesthetic activities. She also likes to sing and remembers tunes and jingles in the proper sequence.

The grade-level team decided to begin with one strategy and that would be the use of increased manipulatives for each of her activities. Karen would be required to manipulate (or move) the objects in the correct order as she spoke about the sequence of the objects. She would work with a peer and also a computerized program that would provide additional practice in sequencing. Her teacher indicated that at the computer table on the side of the classroom there is a small table that would allow Karen to manipulate block patterns and various shapes in front of the computer as she was looking at the problems on the computer screen. She could also use the blocks in front of her to simulate the picture shown on the screen while verbalizing each one of the sequences as she selects them. Her teacher indicated that he would monitor Karen to make sure that she was using the manipulatives accurately and verbalizing her actions.

Exhibit 4.1 is a list of some of the sequencing interventions recommended for K–2 students.

IMPLEMENTATION TIP

The grade-level team (including the special education teacher) discussed a variety of options based on their assessment shown in Exhibit 4.1. Here are additional items they discussed to help them decide on the implementation:

► **IInterventions** may include time, such as duration and frequency (e.g., 20, 30, 45 minutes a day, two times a week, daily); environment (physical location, structure); personnel (teacher, specialist); and grouping (small 1:5 or 1:3, heterogeneous, homogenous). The higher the tier, the smaller the group and the formative assessment (two times a month, weekly, two times a week, daily). The higher the tier, the more frequent the need for assessment to monitor the student's progress. Remember, core Tier 1 provides the research-based instruction with differentiation as needed, based on the pre-assessed needs of the students from a highly qualified teacher during core instruction. Students in Tiers 2–3 require intensified intervention strategies and activities.

► **Strategies** shown are samples of the intentional adult actions that should have the greatest positive impact on student learning, such as the use of visual cues, manipulatives, and prompts. Select the strategy based on the strengths, challenges, and inferences discussed during the meeting.

► **Activities** shown are the actions of the students, such as working with a peer buddy or collaborative teams.

NOTE: This is not intended to be an exhaustive list of possible activities and strategies for this area of content. Typically, there is not a dividing line between some of the tiers. It may be that the strategy or classroom activity will be appropriate for multiple tiers. In some cases, the time, intensity, and duration of a strategy may be modified to suit particular groups or individual students. Read the "How Does It Look" section to see which strategy, activity, and assessment was used by this particular team. Discuss other strategies that may be appropriate based on the scenario.

Reflection: *Karen's teacher is beginning to worry that she will not have enough time in her class of 25 kindergarteners to devote the time to provide manipulatives, visual cues, and prompts for Karen to help her with the sequencing strategies suggested by the grade-level team. What advice would you give her?*

EXHIBIT 4.1	Sample K–2 Sequencing*	

Sample Tiers	Strategies and Activities	Description
2, 3	Use manipulatives (cubes) while counting	
1, 2	Partner or peer buddy while counting	Pair student for a few minutes several times a week with a peer who has developed the sequencing skill already. It does not have to be the same peer each time.
3	Computer practice along with manipulatives	Use computer software for practice but include tangible (manipulative) practice with each screen.
2, 3	Repetition	Student should be prompted to verbally repeat the first and second directions required. Next, do the activity and repeat the direction. Ask student to verbalize to check for understanding before adding another step.
2, 3	Visual cues and prompts	Provide verbal modeling, pictures, or demonstrations during two- or three-step directions.
Additional:		
Additional:		

* Note: This is not meant as an exhaustive list of the instructional strategies, interventions, or activities.

Source: House, 2004

HOW DOES IT LOOK?

Directly following the grade-level team meeting, Karen's teacher, Mr. Stein, decided to begin the new intervention strategy immediately. He would use blocks or various objects while counting in sequence with Karen. He decided to introduce this strategy during her learning station rotations. He noticed that there were three other students who were also having the same difficulty counting in sequence and following multiple-step directions. He said he would try this intervention with all four students during the station rotations. Following that, he decided to monitor the progress of the students through observation. He would allow them to sit at their desks and use the manipulatives, work with a peer buddy, or use the computer system for additional practice.

In addition to the core Tier 1 instructional strategy, Karen's teacher provided an additional station rotation in which Karen received an additional 20 minutes three times a week of instruction in sequencing. As a Tier 3 intervention Karen also received specially designed instruction from the special education teacher to comply with the goals and objectives listed on her IEP.

 HOW IS IT MONITORED?

Mr. Stein decided to use an observation checklist and teacher-made assessments to monitor the progress of Karen and her three classmates who required the additional Tier 1 intervention. The students who are using this system are receiving differentiation through the use of manipulatives and a skill practice computer program. They are using the same content of counting and recognizing things in order as their peers during class but with more manipulative, tactile, or kinesthetic opportunities and more time and practice. They are not being pulled out, and they are not receiving services from additional personnel to accomplish this particular goal of sequencing and learning to follow multistep directions.

The team determined that this method should continue for approximately two weeks. At the next meeting, the observation and assessment notes would be analyzed to see if the time, duration, frequency, or intensity of the intervention needed to be adjusted.

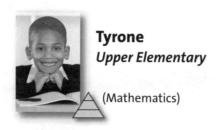

Tyrone
Upper Elementary

(Mathematics)

Tyrone is a student who loves school. His favorite subjects are science and physical education. He indicated that he likes the experiments and hands-on activities in his science class. Even though his reading is not on grade level, he is able to follow the teacher's directions and watch her visuals and demonstrations without a problem. His teacher, Ms. Santana, has a bachelor's degree in science and uses every opportunity to help her students develop the skills needed to understand the content. Tyrone also has a vivid imagination and is intrigued by the science content. Ms. Santana has concerns regarding his progress in school. Tyrone has exhibited a number of splintered skills in mathematics.

At the end of one of his class sessions, Tyrone confided to Ms. Santana that he loves school but finds it difficult to grasp basic math concepts. Currently, he is struggling with division in class. He has not yet learned multiplication facts. Tyrone said he simply can't understand what everyone else sees when they are making determinations of which numbers belong in each column of the problem. Ms. Santana did notice that Tyrone tends to wander around during class—sharpens his pencil, briefly chats with peers, looks for items supposedly lost from his backpack, and finds ways to avoid math assignments whenever possible. He recently admitted that he procrastinates because he just doesn't understand what to do and is too shy to raise his hand for help in front of his peers. He receives services for special education and indicated that he believes his general education classmates look at him and treat him differently. There is a mathematics goal on his IEP, but he is not making adequate progress. Ms. Santana decided to share this information at the grade-level team meeting the next morning. She was delighted that Tyrone's special education teacher would be in attendance at the meeting tomorrow as well. The special education teacher is split between three grade levels and routinely attends the grade-level team meeting twice each month, once during the third-grade and once during the fourth-grade session. The bulk of his caseload for special education this semester is in the third and fourth grades. He uses a consultation model to assist teachers on the fourth-grade team who have a few students with IEPs. The students are responding as expected to research-based intervention strategies in their classes. Currently, these students do not require a high level of intensity. The instructional coach and assistant principal will also be in attendance during the 45-minute grade-level team meeting.

As planned, the grade-level team met the next morning and again reviewed the universal mathematics assessment given to all students, including Tyrone, at the beginning of the school year. The team also reviewed the curriculum-based end-of-unit assessments and teacher-made common formative assessments for the fourth-grade students in basic math facts for the past two weeks. The team analyzed the strengths and challenges, made inferences regarding the results, and determined root causes of the problem for several students, including Tyrone.

Tyrone is struggling to learn basic multiplication facts. The fourth-grade teachers noted that several students in their classes had difficulty with basic multiplication facts. All of the students, including Tyrone, seemed quite proficient with multiples of 2, 5, 10, and 11 but struggled with the other numbers. According to the fourth-grade pacing guide, all of the students should be proficient in division and beginning at least three operations of fractions.

Tyrone's IEP indicates that he is eligible as a student with a specific learning disability in the area of mathematics. After collecting the pre-assessment data, the grade-level team said that Tyrone had good addition skills but continued to have difficulty remembering basic multiplication facts. Tyrone mentioned that he did not remember learning multiplication facts in school. The fourth-grade team decided that Tyrone would work with two online programs: IXL (www.IXL.com) and the National Library of Virtual Manipulatives (http://nlvm.usu.edu/).

The entire class is currently learning long-division problems. Tyrone will be allowed to use a multiplication chart in order to continue learning the multiplication facts along with the steps of division. In addition to the classroom activities, the special education teacher worked out a schedule with the teachers to push-in the math class during work station rotations an average of 30 minutes a day, three times a week, to work with Tyrone and a few other classmates who are also having difficulty with multiplication facts and division. The team mentioned that frequently the instructional methods used for students who are eligible for special education services also benefit general education students who require targeted instruction that more closely addresses their learning styles and modality, optimal group size, and time format. The sessions at the work stations consisted of four or five students and one teacher.

Exhibit 4.2 lists some of the interventions used for multiplication facts and division.

> **Reflection:** *Select one intervention strategy from the list shown below and describe how you might be able to implement it in your class for a student with a profile similar to Tyrone's. Or describe another strategy that you have used that has proven successful.*

 IMPLEMENTATION TIP

The grade-level team (including the special education teacher) discussed a variety of options based on their assessment shown in Exhibit 4.2. Here are additional items they discussed to help them decide on the implementation:

▶ **Interventions** may include time, such as duration and frequency (e.g., 20, 30, 45 minutes a day, two times a week, daily); environment (physical location, structure); personnel (teacher, specialist); and grouping (small 1:5 or 1:3, heterogeneous, homogenous). The higher the tier, the smaller the group and the formative assessment (two times a month, weekly, two times a week, daily). The higher the tier, the more frequent the need for assessment to monitor the student's progress. Remember, core Tier 1 provides the research-based instruction with differentiation as needed, based on the pre-assessed needs of the students from a highly qualified teacher during core instruction. Students in Tiers 2–3 require intensified intervention strategies and activities.

▶ **Strategies** shown are samples of the intentional adult actions that should have the greatest positive impact on student learning, such as the use of technology (software and programs). Select the strategy based on the strengths, challenges, and inferences discussed during the meeting.

▶ **Activities** shown are the actions of the students, such as flash cards for additional practice, or targeted assignments during, before, or after school tutorials.

NOTE: This is not intended to be an exhaustive list of possible activities and strategies for this area of content. Typically, there is not a dividing line between some of the tiers. It may be that the strategy or classroom activity will be appropriate for multiple tiers. In some cases, the time, intensity, and duration of a strategy may be modified to suit particular groups or individual students. Read the "How Does It Look" section to see which strategy, activity, and assessment was used by this particular team. Discuss other strategies that may be appropriate based on the scenario.

 HOW DOES IT LOOK?

Tyrone's teacher decided that the easiest way to introduce the manipulatives for Tyrone and his classmates would be to use a station-rotation teaching session. On Mondays, Wednesdays, and Fridays for approximately 30 minutes, the special education teacher helped with the station rotation. The classroom teacher began a direct instruction lesson with a small group of approximately four to five students and explained to the students how they would use the manipulatives. Next, the students rotated to the paraprofessional for follow-up and additional guided practice and then continued with independent practice. Additionally, the students were introduced by the classroom teacher to computer programs. The National Library of Virtual Manipulatives (http://nlvm.usu.edu/) allows students to use a variety of manipulatives in multiplication in order to practice their facts. Another program IXL (www.IXL.com) provides additional practice for students using multiplication facts. When these students used the drill and practice program on the computer, they were also required to write their problems in a strategies notebook. The program also allowed the classroom teacher the opportunity to see the students' progress. At least once a week for approximately 20 minutes, the special education teacher and the general education teacher teamed to introduce new concepts to the entire class. The students agreed that this was their favorite time in class. The teachers worked out a collaborative plan that provided all of the students with rich lessons that included visuals, lots of examples, vocabulary games, and exemplars. Occasionally, the two teachers would divide the class in half (homogeneous or heterogeneous groups) to provide small sessions of direct instruction. They worked well together and found that over time it only took a few minutes to plan together. The students respected both teachers equally, which provided a positive cooperative learning environment. Tyrone's general education teacher asked the physical education teacher if he would try an intervention during his fourth-grade class with all of the students. Rather than counting from 1 to 20 while performing jumping jacks, push-ups, and sit-ups, for example, the students were required to count by multiples of 3, 4, 6, 7, 8, 9, and 12. The physical education

EXHIBIT 4.2 **Sample Grades 4–6 Multiplication Facts and Division***

Sample Tiers	Strategies and Activities	Description
2, 3	Flash cards/visual practice with peers	Practice multiplication tables with a peer. Use as a homework assignment as well. Use the new fact (e.g., six) in numerous ways throughout the day. Pay special attention to having students notice the numbers and patterns whenever possible in their environment.
2, 3	www.IXL.com (computer program practice)	Opportunities for additional drill and practice outside of the general lesson online. There are numerous computerized software programs that may provide sustainable practice through interesting graphics and sequential applications.
2, 3	National Library of Virtual Manipulatives http://nlvm.usu.edu/en/nav/vlibrary.html (online manipulatives)	This Web site may be reached through http://free.ed.gov as well. These manipulatives may be created as plastic or cardstock. If the computer is used for additional drill and practice, make sure that it is being carefully monitored for accuracy and not just random selection. For example, periodically ask the student to justify their selection or to explain their procedures prior to pressing the enter key.
2, 3	Kinesthetic activity during PE class	Physical education, art, and music teachers can integrate mathematics into their lessons when possible. The core teacher should let them know the math facts or the unit that is being taught.
3	Thirty minutes, three times a week, with special education teacher (push-in)	The number of minutes of specially designed instruction provided by the special educator is designated by the IEP team members.
2, 3	Patterning exercises	Provide patterns on paper, in the room, or through exercises that allow students to see groups and patterns of objects and numbers. Relationships should be considered (e.g., Could this group of three blocks go into five? How many times?)
1, 2, 3	Create charts (exemplars)	Allow students to create charts of exemplars with their written explanations (student-friendly language) of how to solve the problem.
1, 2, 3	Math journal	Students maintain a journal of new problem-solving methods; for example, how they in their own words solved the problem. Language experience approach can be used here for students who struggle with writing. In this strategy, the student dictates the information to a teacher, volunteer, paraprofessional, or interventionist for the journal.
Additional:		
Additional:		
Additional:		

* Note: This is not meant as an exhaustive list of the instructional strategies, interventions, or activities discussed by the team.

Source: Stein, Silbert, and Carnine, 1997.

teacher decided that he would have no problem asking the students to use this form of counting. On the first day, he began with the number 3 and asked the students to count by 3s as they were doing their warm-up exercises. He checked in frequently with the fourth-grade team to decide which numbers should be practiced next. These exercises seemed to be working quite well, and the students enjoyed doing them. In addition to assistance from the general education teacher, technology, and the physical education teacher, Tyrone also received specially designed instruction based on the goals and objectives listed on his IEP to ensure access to the general education curriculum for his required math skills.

 ## HOW IS IT MONITORED?

Ms. Santana, Tyrone's general education teacher, asked him to keep a chart indicating each multiplication fact he was successfully able to learn with 100 percent accuracy. It was easy for Tyrone to keep track of his own progress. The chart also provided a quick visual display of the multiplication facts. Other students in class could track their own progress as well. This proved very helpful for the paraprofessional and physical education teacher so they could assist the students quickly by reviewing the students' charts. The classroom teacher also printed copies of the results of the computer programs that Tyrone and his classmates had used. This information was shared on a bimonthly basis with the grade-level team. In a very short period of time, Tyrone was able to learn his multiplication facts. The additional time (direct instruction), practice (computer), advance organizers, manipulatives, recognition of patterns, and specially designed instruction helped Tyrone and his classmates to understand the concepts and to catch up to their peers in division.

Kelsey
Secondary

(Reading)

Kelsey's favorite subject in school is physical education. Unfortunately, because of her grades in language arts, social studies, and science, she is unable to qualify for the freshman volleyball team. Her special education case manager, Ms. Yang, has noted that Kelsey's academic scores are severely impacted by her low reading level of 3.0. Kelsey is a very self-confident, enthusiastic, and charismatic student. She has strong skills in mathematics but continues to struggle with reading. During the ninth-grade content department team meeting, the science teacher mentioned that when she gives Kelsey science homework to read (e.g., one chapter), Kelsey takes almost two hours to read 10 pages, and her comprehension of the material is very poor. Her social studies teacher expressed the same concern. In the past, Ms. Yang had suggested additional time for assignments and shorter modified assignments for homework that do not require reading entire chapters each evening. Kelsey's social studies and science teachers commented that these shortened homework assignments would hinder Kelsey's ability to take adequate notes during class and would limit her understanding of the course content. They expressed frustration with simply shortening her assignments and said they felt more attention should be focused on teaching Kelsey to read. The teachers noted that an additional challenge was Kelsey's poor background knowledge and vocabulary in social studies and science. The secondary teachers were at a loss as to how to help Kelsey because they have a very strict pacing guide and must keep on schedule. The teachers did observe that Kelsey has a good memory and appears to do well if the information is presented to her verbally. But she struggles to take notes and listen to class lectures at the same time. The state-mandated assessments require proficiency in English, mathematics, science, and social studies. At this point, Kelsey has been able to pass all of her math proficiency assessments with the IEP modification that, during the assessment, the directions for math may be read to her.

The ninth-grade Data Team members knew Kelsey was a popular student on campus but was also a student who struggled with reading. They decided to use a joint intervention for the next two weeks to see how Kelsey responded. They chose to use technology because Kelsey was very proficient with various technological devices such as Facebook and Twitter. When she used these Web sites, however, her spelling was very poor, but it was evident that Kelsey was anxious to communicate with her friends. The team decided that this was a strength for Kelsey because she would be able to use technology in a variety of ways throughout her life.

Rather than eliminating the science and social studies homework chapters, Kelsey would be able to use an electronic reader so that she could hear the content of each of the chapters. She would be required to record reflections or answer specific questions after each paragraph or after a couple of sentences. This would be done electronically using the WYNN Reader (http://ww2.fredomscientific.com/lsg/products/wynn.asp) or on paper. The English language arts teacher places the majority of his lessons on PowerPoint for his class. Ms. Yang decided to use the electronic program Camtasia to record the teacher's voice during the presentation of the PowerPoint slides to the class and have that available for Kelsey and other students who might need to hear and/or see the information again. Kelsey is eligible for intensive special education services in reading and would continue to see her special education teacher according to her IEP for reading on a daily basis. Rather than a computer software program at home, it was decided by the special education teacher, general education teacher, Kelsey, and Kelsey's parents that it would be more beneficial for Kelsey to use the resource room for additional assistance in reading based on the determination designated in the IEP. The team decided that it would be most helpful to provide frequent short pre-assessments to help target specific reading skills needed to help Kelsey close the gap in reading while still learning the course content of ninth grade. Exhibit 4.3 lists some of the interventions discussed during the team meeting.

> **Reflection:** *The department team decided to invite Kelsey to their meeting. They wanted to know a little more about her before implementing the strategies. If you were part of the team, what three questions would you ask her?*

IMPLEMENTATION TIP

The English department team (including the special education teacher) discussed a variety of options based on their assessment shown in Exhibit 4.3. Here are additional items they discussed to help them decide on the implementation:

▶ **Interventions** may include time, such as duration and frequency (e.g., 20, 30, 45 minutes a day, two times a week, daily); environment (physical location, structure); personnel (teacher, specialist); and grouping (small 1:5 or 1:3, heterogeneous, homogenous). The higher the tier, the smaller the group and the formative assessment (two times a month, weekly, two times a week, daily). The higher the tier, the more frequent the need for assessment to monitor the student's progress. Remember, core Tier 1 provides the research-based instruction with differentiation as needed, based on the pre-assessed needs of the students from a highly qualified teacher during core instruction. Students in Tiers 2–3 require intensified intervention strategies and activities.

▶ **Strategies** shown are samples of the intentional adult actions that should have the greatest positive impact on student learning, such as the use of visuals, hands-on activities, technology programs, or teacher-generated programs in Camtasia. Select the strategy based on the strengths, challenges, and inferences discussed during the meeting.

▶ **Activities** shown are the actions of the student, such as maintaining a reading notebook or journal filled with prompts for Quick Write reflections.

NOTE: This is not intended to be an exhaustive list of possible activities and strategies for this area of content. Typically, there is not a dividing line between some of the tiers. It may be that the strategy or classroom activity will be appropriate for multiple tiers. In some cases, the time, intensity, and duration of a strategy may be modified to suit particular groups or individual students. Read the "How Does It Look" section to see which strategy, activity, and assessment was used by this particular team. Discuss other strategies that may be appropriate based on the scenario.

EXHIBIT 4.3 **Sample Ninth-Grade Reading**

Sample Tiers	Strategies and Activities	Description
3	Electronic reader (WYNN or Kurzweil)	Windows XP, WYNN Reader (Freedom Scientific), and Kurzweil are a few examples of content-activated readers that will assist students in hearing the text of their curriculum materials that have been scanned.
3	Camtasia (computer lessons)	Recorded PowerPoint and computer lessons (sound and visuals).
2, 3	Vocabulary skill development (special education teacher)	Provide alternative teaching activities to front-load vocabulary using specially designed instruction with graphic organizers and preprinted lecture notes.
2, 3	Direct instruction	Explicit reading strategies with frequent assessment and monitoring within the context of the course content.
2, 3	Increased use of visuals and hands-on activities	Social studies and science demonstrations, modeling, video clips (when possible), hands-on activities.
Additional:		
Additional:		
Additional:		

Source: House, 2004.

 ## HOW DOES IT LOOK?

The English language arts, science, and social studies teachers began the new plan immediately. A meeting was held after school with the science teacher, social studies teacher, special education teacher, Kelsey, and her parents to explain the new intervention strategy. Her parents were very excited to hear that Kelsey would be able to obtain the course content by using the electronic reader on their home computer. Kelsey's mother indicated that her daughter is often on the computer after school and on weekends, and it would be great for her to use it for academic work. Kelsey also thought that this would help her get through the information a lot quicker, and she believed she would understand ninth-grade-level content if it was read to her electronically. The Kurzweil and WYNN readers also have colored screens, modified pacing, and opportunities to learn vocabulary and take notes in an interactive manner on the computer within the text. Kelsey's English language arts teacher indicated that it would be necessary for Kelsey to keep a notebook of new vocabulary. He would also connect with her special education teacher for each of the subject areas and develop ways to use the new vocabulary, not just for the core subject areas but also in other areas of her life.

HOW IS IT MONITORED?

Kelsey's special education teacher, Ms. Yang, indicated that she would be the case manager for monitoring Kelsey's progress in language arts, social studies, and science. The team agreed to formally meet on a bimonthly basis as a grade-level team. Ms. Yang would check with Kelsey's teachers on a weekly basis to make sure that Kelsey was making progress as expected. Kelsey's mother and father also agreed to help monitor her use of the computer programs at home to make sure that she completed reading each of her electronic assignments. Kelsey told the team that for the first time she felt that she had a real opportunity to catch up to her classmates, and perhaps she would be able to qualify at some point in the near future for the junior volleyball team. Her motivation is high.

HOW HAVE YOU THOUGHT ABOUT?

Students with special education needs require instructional intervention strategies that address their individual differences and learning conditions. This teaching involves deliberate and systematically monitored planning that addresses learning procedures, adapted environments, and accessible settings to help students achieve in the school and community. Common needs include learning challenges, emotional and behavioral disorders, and physical disabilities.

As you reflect on the three students in the special education scenarios, think about how their situation applies to your teaching and learning. Consider these questions:

► How are visual and auditory strategies helpful for special education students? What types do you use in your classroom to promote learning?

► What is the role of elective and cultural arts teachers in supporting your efforts with the core content standards? How can they provide additional reinforcement of basic skills and knowledge?

► How can technology be used to support the needs of special education students?

CHAPTER FIVE

Gifted and Talented Scenarios

 GIFTED SNAPSHOT

What: Students designated by the district as gifted will receive Tier 1 core instruction along with their peers from a highly qualified, general-education teacher. Instruction will be differentiated to address their pre-assessed needs as gifted learners. Districts may provide additional Specially Designed Instruction (SDI) from the special education teacher (or licensed teacher of the gifted) in the general-education class (push-in model) or in a lab or resource learning center (pull-out model) as designated by the area of need if the student has an IEP. Secondary students may be assigned to an additional class for targeted or intensive instruction. Services and eligibility for gifted and talented students differ widely from state to state. Some states do not recognize gifted for special education and some states will not consider eligibility until third grade.

Who: Tier 2 instructional gifted intervention may be provided by a highly qualified, general-education teacher, qualified specialist, or the licensed special education teacher (if permitted by the state). The determination of who may provide the direct service is a district decision. Specific minutes of supplemental instruction is listed on the IEP. If the student is not classified as special education for gifted, the grade level or content team may determine the levels of intensity of services based on the pre-assessed needs.

Where: Instruction in Tiers 1, 2, and 3 typically takes place in a collaborative general education classroom. In a few cases however, students are pulled out for specific training as needed by a gifted education specialist during Tiers 2 and 3.

When: Intensity time, duration and frequency of the targeted or intensive instructional intervention, and progress monitoring may be determined by the IEP, grade-level, or content-team members based on the pre-assessed needs of the student. The core instruction of Tier 1 should not be supplanted. In this case, the goal is to ensure appropriate access to the general education curriculum.

79

Why: Gifted students may receive a variety of services based on present levels of performance in one or more areas. If the student qualifies for special education as gifted, the licensed gifted education teacher will provide SDI based on the IEP. For students designated as gifted but not considered special education by the State will still receive supplemental and intensive services from the general education or other designated highly qualified teacher as needed.

Lydia
Primary

(Mathematics)

Lydia is a rambunctious five-year-old. When asked her age, Lydia will tell you that she is 10! Frankly, at times she does appear mature enough in class to be a much older youngster. She attended a private community preschool program. She knows her way around campus and is always on the move. Lydia can frequently be heard telling other students what to do. She often speaks for her classmates and corrects their work. She absolutely loves to play games but becomes enraged when she doesn't win. Lydia truly enjoys learning new things at school and thinks her teacher, Ms. Martinez, is great. Lydia is very social and is learning to speak Mandarin Chinese and Spanish from two of her classmates.

Both of Lydia's parents are scientists and work for a scientific government laboratory. She is their only child, and they are very proud of her but admit that she does tend to pout and become sullen when full attention is not devoted to her. Lydia's teacher finds Lydia quite challenging. Ms. Martinez reported last week to her grade-level team that Lydia is "off the charts" on the universal assessment that was administered within the first few months of school. Lydia is operating at two grade levels above kindergarten in mathematics, science, social studies, reading, and language arts. The leader of the team smiled and asked Ms. Martinez to define in objective terms the expression "off the charts" so that everyone on the team would have a clear picture of what she meant. Ms. Martinez is beginning her second year as a teacher. She indicated that Lydia and four of her classmates are scoring up to three grade levels above all of the other students. The scores for the majority of the students at the K–6 elementary school are at or above grade level. They have the largest concentration of identified gifted students in the state.

Ms. Martinez mentioned that although Lydia is two years above grade level in reading, social studies, and science, she is actually three years above grade level in mathematics and completes all of her math assignments faster than her classmates. Ms. Martinez frequently asks Lydia to tutor her classmates or to do more work. Lydia complains to her parents that school is boring, and she's starting to get tired of tutoring her classmates in math. She doesn't seem to be interested in learning new things any longer. Now Lydia and a couple of her classmates just want to play games in class. They are starting to refuse to do some assignments and are frequently pointing out when others make mistakes. Lydia has taken a superior attitude and is beginning to verbalize the belief that her teacher is unable to provide appropriate work for her. Lydia's parents called to say that Ms. Martinez needed to develop a plan to help Lydia instead of using her as a teaching assistant in class or giving her more kindergarten math assignments.

In Lydia's state, students cannot be considered for gifted program services until the third grade. But based on Lydia's academic performance, Ms. Martinez is confident that she would qualify. Ms. Martinez explained to the grade-level team that she was concerned she was not meeting Lydia's needs and asked the team for help. They looked at Lydia's work samples and the teacher's anecdotal notes as well as the work of two other students in class. They analyzed the strengths and challenges shown in each sample. The team determined that Lydia needed to have differentiated intervention strategies that would allow her to move forward and continue to grow academically. The mathematics coach in attendance at the team meeting indicated that there are several interventions that should help Ms. Martinez address the needs of the students who are significantly above grade level in math. The coach indicated that it is important to carefully identify student needs. From Ms. Martinez's notes and Lydia's work samples, it appears that Lydia learns new math concepts very quickly, is curious about math, and is persistent in problem solving. The coach indicated that she feels Lydia will benefit from additional instruction outside the regular curriculum. She mentioned that due to her maturity as well as her high cognitive development, Lydia should be considered for accelerated instruction.

Lydia does not seem to have problems understanding math concepts and memorizes the algorithms needed to solve the math problems at higher grade levels. Her abstract reasoning and application skills are quite remarkable for her age. The coach volunteered to provide an assessment to the students identified for the Tier 2 targeted instruction to make sure that they have a good understanding of the underlying concepts of math.

Ms. Martinez suggested simply placing these four students in the third-grade classroom for math instruction. The grade-level team said that that was a possibility but felt that merely moving Lydia and her advanced peers to a higher grade level might not provide the help they need in developing critical and creative thinking. But Ms. Martinez was concerned that having the students remain with the same kindergarten structure had not proved successful and that the pacing was just too slow. The math coach suggested using learning centers in class that provided a variety of opportunities to work with age-appropriate and skill-matched logic problems and math puzzles.

The math coach suggested that the team investigate different materials that include advanced content with a problem-solving focus. She explained to Ms. Martinez that her previous strategy of giving Lydia more of the same assignments and designating her as class tutor, should not continue. The team felt that the students could remain in the class but would need to be challenged beyond the standard curriculum. To avoid slow pacing and boredom, the team decided that Ms. Martinez should try flexible grouping and flexible pacing. During the small homogeneous group setting, the teacher would facilitate the discussion and make sure that the students had an opportunity to explore and share their thinking with their peers. The groups and pacing would be determined by the pre-assessment. Learning stations within the general classroom structure would be formed for each unit of instruction. Ms. Martinez indicated that performance seems to fluctuate throughout the semester, so students may move in and out of these groups based on their response to the weekly formative assessments. The flexible grouping will allow the teacher an opportunity to use a variety of materials that include appropriate advanced content with a problem-solving focus. The team agreed that this form of differentiated instruction will help provide interest and a comfortable yet challenging environment for the kindergartners who have exceeded the general core instruction. The math coach volunteered to look for additional materials, for example, from the National Council of Teachers of Mathematics (NCTM) and the National Research Center on the Gifted and Talented (NRC/GT) from the University of Connecticut.

Some of the mathematics interventions/strategies are shown in Exhibit 5.1.

> **Reflection:** *What programs or policies does your school have in place to address the needs of accelerated learners in pre-K through second grade?*

IMPLEMENTATION TIP

The grade-level team discussed a variety of options based on their assessment shown in Exhibit 5.1. Here are additional items they discussed to help them decide on the implementation:

- ► **Interventions** may include time, such as duration and frequency (e.g., 20, 30, 45 minutes a day, two times a week, daily); environment (physical location, structure); personnel (teacher, specialist); and grouping (small 1:5 or 1:3, heterogeneous, homogenous). The higher the tier, the smaller the group and the formative assessment (two times a month, weekly, two times a week, daily). The higher the tier, the more frequent the need for assessment to monitor the student's progress. Remember, core Tier 1 provides the research-based instruction with differentiation as needed, based on the pre-assessed needs of the students from a highly qualified teacher during core instruction. Students in Tiers 2–3 require intensified intervention strategies and activities.

- ► **Strategies** shown are samples of the intentional adult actions that should have the greatest positive impact on student learning, such as the use of learning stations and learning centers. Select the strategy based on the strengths, challenges, and inferences discussed during the meeting.

- ► **Activities** shown are the actions of the students, such as working in small groups to provide direct instruction.

NOTE: This is not intended to be an exhaustive list of possible activities and strategies for this area of content. Typically, there is not a dividing line between some of the tiers. It may be that the strategy or classroom activity will be appropriate for multiple tiers. In some cases, the time, intensity, and duration of a strategy may be modified to suit particular groups or individual students. Read the "How Does It Look" section to see which strategy, activity, and assessment was used by this particular team. Discuss other strategies that may be appropriate based on the scenario.

EXHIBIT 5.1   **Sample K–2 Mathematics**

Sample Tiers	Strategies and Activities	Description
2, 3	Flexible grouping	Students will be assigned to small collaborative homogeneous groups. The groups will change based on pre- and post-assessments.
2, 3	Pre- and post-assessments	In addition to the universal screening, a short formative assessment will be used on a weekly basis with observation of student performance between assessments.
1, 2, 3	Learning centers	Learning centers will provide opportunities for independent practice with inquiry-based activities.
1, 2, 3	Learning stations	Students will be able to move to 3–4 learning stations that will give them the opportunity not only to work together but also to rotate to targeted, differentiated direct instruction and guided practice.
2, 3	Specific materials	The teacher can use scientifically research-based instructional materials specifically designed for gifted and talented students.
Additional:		
Additional:		
Additional:		

Sources: The National Research Center on the Gifted and Talented (NRC/GT), University of Connecticut, http://www.gifted.uconn.edu/nrcgt.html; National Council of Teachers of Mathematics (NCTM), http://www.nctm.org/

 HOW DOES IT LOOK?

In order to provide appropriate math lessons for Lydia and the other students requiring targeted assistance for advanced mathematics, Ms. Martinez administered a short pre-assessment for the next small unit of study. After the results were scored and analyzed, she decided to develop two learning centers. The math coach helped her locate several software programs that were differentiated to meet the needs of all students in her class. There are four computers in the classroom and 25 kindergarten students. Students learned to work on the computers in pairs. Another learning center developed for the students during math was for inquiry learning. Students were assigned boxes with engaging inquiry activities designed to challenge students to develop skills in investigating, predicting, and hypothesizing. During flex group sessions and learning stations, Ms. Martinez took the opportunity to work with the students in homogeneous groupings (based on the ongoing assessments) to provide research-based, skill-appropriate materials, accelerated learning, and direct instruction.

 HOW IS IT MONITORED?

Fortunately, it appears that Lydia is responding well to the instructional math strategies. Interestingly, she also seems calmer and more focused in class. Her parents called to say that they are relieved to know their daughter's individual needs are being met. This is good news, but Ms. Martinez knew that she would need to provide documentation to her team to help form her next steps. She developed an easy-to-use progress monitoring form (see Appendix G). Ms. Martinez uses this form to monitor Lydia's response to the interventions and has found it helpful to make reports to the grade-level team and to Lydia's parents as well. She decided to use the same form for her other students who are receiving targeted or intensive interventions. She expressed excitement that she would be able to document and monitor her students in such a professional manner.

Kim
Upper Elementary

(Writing)

Kim is a very introspective eight-year-old student. He excelled in all of his classes last year, and it was determined that the best plan was to promote him to the next grade. He is one year younger than his peers and doing well academically. Kim has not really developed friendships with his classmates, but his teacher is not worried; she feels he is a well-adjusted student. His hobbies are model cars and airplanes. He plans to travel the world and be an archaeologist. Kim stated that he watched a television special from National Geographic that introduced him to this possible career. He enjoys reading nonfiction books, especially those books that describe other countries in South America, Europe, and Asia. His parents also indicated at the last parent conference that they purchase items for him primarily at the National Geographic store, the local museum, and the Discovery Channel store online. Kim maintains a personal journal and writes every day. In his spare time at school and at home, Kim can be found writing in his journal. During the summer, the local library helped him publish a set of short stories and poetry. He actually sold enough to buy a new bicycle.

During the last grade-level team meeting, his teacher, Ms. Tollison, was asked by her colleagues what intervention strategies she would use to make sure that Kim's skill in writing was still nurtured while his classmates continued to learn basic writing skills as described in the state standards. The team reviewed Kim's universal screening, analyzed his strengths and challenges, and made several inferences.

The team determined that Kim should continue to maintain an interactive journal and continue attending lessons with his fourth-grade peers. They also felt that to meet Kim's individual needs, he should have the opportunity to work with a university English language arts tutor once a week. Ms. Tollison is pleased with his response to the differentiated instruction provided in class but also believes that Kim could achieve more with the additional intervention of the after-school tutoring program.

Kim was also enrolled in a cross-district pen pal program that matched similar students in an ongoing monitored series of writing activities. Students shared poems and short stories and became friends through the Internet writing club. Kim was partnered with a fellow nonfiction writing enthusiast from a sixth-grade class. His vocabulary, sentence construction, style, and production have improved tremendously. He is hoping next year to have a pen pal from South America.

In addition to his fourth-grade lessons in writing, Kim created a book club at the school. Students in grades 3–6 met once a month during lunch and shared short stories with each other that they had written outside of class. One story each month was selected to be published in the school newspaper. Kim found these opportunities to expand and enhance his personal interests intriguing. His teacher, Ms. Tollison, continued to look for additional learning activities that would motivate Kim to excel in writing.

> **Reflection:** *A teacher was overheard questioning why the school spent time and resources on students like Kim who were already proficient in content and skills. Based on what you know about RTI, what would your response to that teacher be?*

Exhibit 5.2 describes a few of the writing strategies suggested by the team following an analysis of Kim's pre-assessment results.

 IMPLEMENTATION TIP

The grade-level team discussed a variety of options based on their assessment shown in Exhibit 5.2. Here are additional items they discussed to help them decide on the implementation:

► **Interventions** may include time, such as duration and frequency (e.g., 20, 30, 45 minutes a day, two times a week, daily); environment (physical location, structure); personnel (teacher, specialist); and grouping (small 1:5 or 1:3, heterogeneous, homogenous). The higher the tier, the smaller the group and the formative assessment (two times a month, weekly, two times a week, daily). The higher the tier, the more frequent the need for assessment to monitor the student's progress. Remember, core Tier 1 provides the research-based instruction with differentiation as needed, based on the pre-assessed needs of the students from a highly qualified teacher during core instruction. Students in Tiers 2–3 require intensified intervention strategies and activities.

► **Strategies** shown in the chart below are samples of the intentional adult actions that should have the greatest positive impact on student learning, such as the creation of pen pal opportunities with appropriate supervision and explicit instructions. Select the strategy based on the strengths, challenges, and inferences discussed during the meeting.

► **Activities** shown in the chart below are the actions of the students, such as the opportunity to publish or display work and share reflection with peers.

NOTE: This is not intended to be an exhaustive list of possible activities and strategies for this area of content. Typically, there is not a dividing line between some of the tiers. It may be that the strategy or classroom activity will be appropriate for multiple tiers. In some cases, the time, intensity, and duration of a strategy may be modified to suit particular groups or individual students. Read the "How Does It Look" section to see which strategy, activity, and assessment was used by this particular team. Discuss other strategies that may be appropriate based on the scenario.

 HOW DOES IT LOOK?

Kim is a very independent student who has already developed a personal journal. Ms. Tollison explained to Kim that she would like to occasionally write comments in his journal as well so that he could receive feedback regarding some of his statements. It would not be graded but could help to facilitate deeper thinking on some of the issues, questions, or concerns that he writes about in the journal. Kim told Ms. Tollison that he would really like to see her comments and believes it will help him learn even more. Kim was very excited to learn that he would be paired with a sixth-grade pen pal in another school across the district. They could also communicate via Skype on a monthly basis. Ms. Tollison was excited that he could use technology. Kim was beginning to learn a publishing program in class during his computer-center time and has begun typing his stories to sell. Kim was enthusiastic about his new writing activities. Ms. Tollison noticed an almost immediate improvement in his writing. She noticed that his motivation seemed to increase, and he spent more time writing on a daily basis.

EXHIBIT 5.2 **Sample Fourth-Grade Writing**

Sample Tiers	Strategies and Activities	Description
2, 3	Maintain an interactive journal	Students use a composition book to write their feelings, experiences, or responses to prompts. In this case, the student kept a journal of his responses to the nonfiction books that he read each week.
2, 3	Develop a cross-classroom, school, district, state, country, or world pen pal	Students may use letter writing, e-mail, or blogs to communicate with pen pals on a variety of topics.
1, 2, 3	Provide an opportunity to share materials	Student clubs are formed around writing interests as a forum to share their writing; for example, poetry clubs, short story clubs, clubs for writing plays. Ultimately work can be selected for publication in the local school or community newspaper.
Additional:		
Additional:		
Additional:		

Source: Literacy and Information Communication System (LINCS) http://lincs.ed.gov

 HOW IS IT MONITORED?

Ms. Tollison had a meeting with Kim to explain the goal of helping him move forward with his writing skills at an advanced level. She enlisted Kim's help in monitoring his progress. Kim agreed to write a short narrative at the end of each week describing or using at least one new skill learned during the week; for example, new poetry forms, use of proper grammar, reduction of redundancy, and use of idioms.

Next, Ms. Tollison suggested that they use a rubric to determine the proficiency of his new writing skills. Kim was taught to self-assess prior to turning in his work. At times, work was peer assessed along with the teacher's assessment, and sometimes common formative writing assessments were collaboratively scored using the rubric with Ms. Tollison's colleagues during the grade-level team meetings.

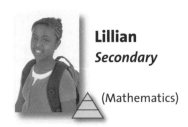

Lillian
Secondary

(Mathematics)

Lillian has great plans for the future. She intends to be an elementary school teacher like her mother. Her father is a dentist, and her older brother is in his first year in college with the goal of becoming an orthodontist. Her hobbies include art and music (she is an excellent harpist and pianist). She also enjoys communicating with friends on Twitter. She logs into her Facebook page daily and loves to chat on her cell phone. Lillian has a solid A average in all of her classes: science, social studies, music, and language arts.

Lillian has qualified as gifted in her school. In the beginning, she did not like the designation because she felt it singled her out and required her to do more assignments than her classmates, with higher expectations from her teachers and parents. She also believes that inadvertently she is being made to wait to learn new things while her classmates get caught up. Sometimes she feels that she is left to her own devices to teach herself. She doesn't always mind, but she does feel that she is not moving forward at the pace she could if given proper intervention.

Lillian's general education mathematics teacher, Mr. Simmons, indicated that he recognizes Lillian is definitely gifted, especially in mathematics. He mentioned to his mathematics department team that he is not trained as a teacher of the gifted and feels that he is not truly meeting Lillian's needs. The campus is small and unable to hire a teacher specifically for students eligible for gifted. Even though Lillian is taking advanced classes in mathematics for her grade level, Mr. Simmons is concerned that he may still not be meeting her needs.

Lillian is a very goal-oriented, mature young student. The mathematics department team suggested that Mr. Simmons review her data and have a discussion with Lillian to talk about her goals. Exhibit 5.3 is a brief transcript of their meeting.

EXHIBIT 5.3 | **Meeting Transcript**

Mr. Simmons:	Hi Lillian. Thank you so much for coming to visit me during your lunch break. This should only take a few minutes.
Lillian:	Sure, no problem. Is everything alright? Is it about my grades?
Mr. Simmons:	Listen, everything is fine. I know you are interested in becoming an elementary school teacher. I think that is going to be fantastic. You have really strong skills in mathematics.
Lillian:	Yes, I really like math. It's easy.
Mr. Simmons:	Do you think sometimes you could be challenged a little more in math?
Lillian:	Well, yes, I probably could.
Mr. Simmons:	Well, I checked with the local community college to see if you could receive credit for attending a class once a week with other students from high schools in the community.
Lillian:	Do you mean like a real college?
Mr. Simmons:	Yes, it could be fun. It's a special program designed to be fun for students that excel in certain subjects, but it also provides a head start with your first steps or college credits. I've already spoken to your parents for permission.
Lillian:	That sounds like it might be fun. I have been a little bored lately.

Reflection: *Mr. Simmons's conversation with Lillian went well. But what would you have done if she said absolutely not to the idea of attending the community college? What other suggestions or steps would you take to help her?*

Mr. Simmons reported back to his department team about the meeting he had had with Lillian and her parents. Lillian is scheduled to begin her mathematics class at the local community college the first week of January for one semester. Apparently, this would take place immediately after school five days a week, and a college van would take her and a few of her classmates to the campus each afternoon. This class would be in place of a high school elective.

The math department felt this would be a great idea. But they indicated that Mr. Simmons should also provide interventions in his general mathematics class to address the needs of all of the students. After reviewing the universal screenings and benchmark assessments for the past few weeks, the team analyzed what he was doing and suggested the following changes in his daily practice (Exhibit 5.4).

 IMPLEMENTATION TIP

The English department team discussed a variety of options based on their assessment shown in Exhibit 5.4. Here are additional items they discussed to help them decide on the implementation:

► **Interventions** may include time, such as duration and frequency (e.g., 20, 30, 45 minutes a day, two times a week, daily); environment (physical location, structure); personnel (teacher, specialist); and grouping (small 1:5 or 1:3, heterogeneous, homogenous). The higher the tier, the smaller the group and the formative assessment (two times a month, weekly, two times a week, daily). The higher the tier, the more frequent the need for assessment to monitor the student's progress. Remember, core Tier 1 provides the research-based instruction with differentiation as needed, based on the pre-assessed needs of the students from a highly qualified teacher during core instruction. Students in Tiers 2–3 require intensified intervention strategies and activities.

► **Strategies** shown are samples of the intentional adult actions that should have the greatest positive impact on student learning, such as the use of accelerated classes or compacted curriculum. Select the strategy based on the strengths, challenges, and inferences discussed during the meeting.

► **Activities** shown are the actions of the student, such as the ability to independently select the products, and create rubrics for their individual core content.

NOTE: This is not intended to be an exhaustive list of possible activities and strategies for this area of content. Typically, there is not a dividing line between some of the tiers. It may be that the strategy or classroom activity will be appropriate for multiple tiers. In some cases, the time, intensity, and duration of a strategy may be modified to suit particular groups or individual students. Read the "How Does It Look" section to see which strategy, activity, and assessment was used by this particular team. Discuss other strategies that may be appropriate based on the scenario.

 HOW DOES IT LOOK?

Mr. Simmons began the new plan immediately. He began with a menu of differentiated skill activities and products from which students could select. The list of products and skill activities were placed on chart paper and posted for all students. Lillian immediately mentioned to Mr. Simmons that the list was not extensive enough and that she had ideas for mathematics products and skill activities that were not on the list. Mr. Simmons was not surprised. He encouraged the class to carefully look at the posted state standards and pacing guide and to actually help him "think outside the box" for additional products and skill activities that could be added to the poster. He also specified that the students would be required to develop

EXHIBIT 5.4	Sample Ninth-Grade Mathematics	
Sample Tiers	**Strategies and Activities**	**Description**
1, 2, 3	Homogeneous cooperative groups	Similar-strength pairs, triads, or quads; jigsaw
1, 2, 3	Individual menu selection	Provide a list of process skill activities at different levels and a list of products that students can select from at least 2–3 times a month. Performance products will require a rubric as well. Once students are provided with an exemplar and the standards, they can write rubrics for approval.
1, 2, 3	Self-selection for group	Students can decide which configuration of study partners they prefer. Lillian typically prefers to work alone.
2, 3	Accelerated classes	Students can attend advanced placement classes, Gifted and Talented (GT) courses, community college courses, or supervised online classes.
Additional:		
Additional:		
Additional:		

Sources: Marzano, 2007;
Literacy and Information Communication System (LINCS) http://lincs.ed.gov

or create an acceptable rubric as necessary for selected performance tasks. Students were given the opportunity to choose whether they wanted to work in pairs, triads, quads, or alone on the menu project. Lillian liked this new plan the best because it allowed her to work with a classmate who works on projects as hard as she does and to occasionally work alone when she has an independent plan she would like to carry out without interruption. She definitely sees room for multiple options.

The highlight of Lillian's day is when she goes to the community college for accelerated mathematics classes. Lillian has met two new friends from another high school in the college class. She is enjoying the experience and feels that she is most excited about the fact that her work will count toward college credits.

 ## HOW IS IT MONITORED?

Mr. Simmons was pleasantly surprised at the new tone in each of his ninth-grade math classes. Initially, he thought that he was targeting Lillian, but he discovered that with just a few steps to differentiate class instruction, all students benefited. They told him they enjoyed it and found the assignments more motivating. He also noticed to his surprise that the students seemed more mature in making their menu selections and in choosing the way they worked. He saw an immediate decrease in disruptive behaviors.

Mr. Simmons tracked Lillian's weekly progress reports at the college and found that she was maintaining an A to A– average. He also began using a progress monitoring form developed by his high school mathematics department to watch the progress of all students in his classes. He reported to the team that he likes the form because it only takes minutes to keep an accurate record. He enjoyed the professional discussions and sharing the results with his colleagues every two weeks. He admitted that initially he truly had his doubts but now understands the power of collaboration.

 ## HOW HAVE YOU THOUGHT ABOUT?

Gifted and talented students show, or have the potential for showing, an exceptional level of performance in intellect, knowledge, concentration, maturity, and creativity. These students possess learning traits that parents and educators may fail to notice. They will comprehend difficult, yet global, concepts in content areas easier than other students and will desire to understand a topic in detail. While advanced in content areas, they often lack social and communication skills. Educators must understand the characteristics of gifted and talented students in order to differentiate appropriately for their specific learning needs.

As you reflect on the three students in the gifted and talented scenarios, think about how their situation applies to your teaching and learning. Consider these questions:

▶ What types of enrichment programs are offered at your school and district for K–12 gifted and talented students? How does each meet their specific learning needs and characteristics of gifted students?

▶ What type of best practices in differentiation do you use in your classroom? How do you enrich the instruction for these students when you have a diverse population of learning needs?

▶ If advanced placement or local community college courses are not available in your community, what other types of options could you design to provide the supplemental enrichment that would support your gifted and talented students?

CHAPTER SIX

English Language Learner Scenarios

 ENGLISH LANGUAGE LEARNERS SNAPSHOT

What: Students designated by the district as English Language Learners (ELLs) will receive Tier 1 core instruction along with their peers from the highly qualified, general-education teacher. Instruction will be differentiated to address their pre-assessed language needs. Districts will provide additional instruction by the licensed teacher of ELLs in the general-education class (push-in model) or in a lab or resource learning center (pull-out model) as designated by the area of need and most effective environment for the instruction. Services and eligibility differ from state to state.

Who: Tier 2 supplemental language instruction will be provided by a highly qualified teacher of ELL.

Where: Instruction in Tiers 1, 2, and 3 typically takes place in a collaborative general education classroom. In a few cases, however, students are pulled out for specific training as needed by a teacher of the ELLs during Tiers 2 and 3.

When: Intensity time, duration, and frequency of the targeted or intensive language instruction may be determined by the grade level or content-team members based on the pre-assessed needs of the student. The core instruction of Tier 1 should not be supplanted. The goal is to provide appropriate language instruction based on the pre-assessed level of language acquisition and to ensure appropriate access to the general education curriculum.

Why: English Language Learners may need a variety of services based on the results of their Language Acquisition Assessment. Students are not placed automatically in Tier 2 or 3. They should be assessed to see which content skills they excel in or need assistance with so they can be provided with program options based on these results.

Aimee
Primary

(Reading Fluency)

Aimee is a bright and eager five-year-old student. She moved to this country when she was three years old from a rural community in China. She does not have siblings. This is her first year in school. When her teacher, Ms. Duncan, learned that Aimee was coming to her class, she quickly consulted a section of CultureGrams (www.culturegrams.com) regarding customs and education in Aimee's native country before speaking with her parents. Ms. Duncan also discussed Aimee's native region in China with the translator, who was from the same rural community. She then scheduled an appointment to meet Aimee's parents. Initially, she was concerned with the need for a translator. Aimee's parents said they would appreciate a translator but did understand basic English. During the parent conference, Ms. Duncan discovered that Aimee's family are physicians who came to the United States on a temporary visa for a special medical training program. They speak Mandarin Chinese at home, but they wanted to make sure that their daughter was proficient in English as well before they returned to China. They said Aimee is adjusting well in the United States and loves nature, animals, music, and drawing. Aimee, along with her classmates, was given a universal screening when she first entered school. As a result of her family's responses on the Home Language Survey, she was also given the Language Acquisition Survey (LAS). The results indicated that she is at the Early Production stage of language acquisition.

Aimee did not attend a preschool program, but she is learning very quickly. She has demonstrated excellent number sense and is doing well in basic arithmetic. She comprehends instructions when visuals, models, demonstrations, and opportunities for practice are provided. Aimee is able to recite songs, number chants, and can count to one hundred.

Aimee is struggling with vocabulary, but Ms. Duncan feels that with differentiated instruction in the class she can help Aimee. Ms. Duncan (through the translator) explained to Aimee's parents that she provides additional time for Aimee's writing assignments and provides models/exemplars and immediate feedback. But she feels that Aimee could still benefit from targeted assistance. Ms. Duncan also described the bimonthly team process to the parents.

Aimee's parents were happy to hear that there was a system in place to help support the achievement of the students in the school. Ms. Duncan explained to them that she would provide frequent assessment of Aimee's progress, analyze her skills, set appropriate goals, implement scientifically research-based strategies with fidelity, and keep documentation of the progress monitoring. She shared with Aimee's parents that this is a method that has benefited the other students on campus and that all students are receiving the academic or behavioral interventions they need to be successful. As they stood up to leave, Aimee's mother and father said they felt confident their daughter was in good hands. They said they were happy to be a part of the team to help educate their daughter.

The next day, Ms. Duncan shared her conversation regarding Aimee with her departmental team's members. There were three other kindergarten teachers who expressed concern as well regarding the vocabulary of their ELLs. After their careful analysis, the team decided they should begin first with implementing high-quality research-based intervention strategies in the general education classroom to see how the students responded.

The team decided first to review basic information regarding ELL instruction from Exhibit 6.1 in order to help them plan lessons, share information with the general educators, and select the appropriate assessment and curriculum.

> **Reflection:** *Which assessment or process does your school or district have in place to determine the student's stage of second-language acquisition? How is this information supported (e.g., professional development)?*

Exhibit 6.2 lists some of the intervention strategies the team discussed for their ELL students.

EXHIBIT 6.1   Stages of Second Language Acquisition

Preproduction	Minimal comprehension Does not verbalize Draws, points Gestures Single answers
Early Production	Limited comprehension One- to two-word responses Uses key words or familiar phrases Uses present-tense verbs
Speech Emergence	Good comprehension Produces simple sentences Grammar and pronunciation errors Misunderstands jokes
Intermediate Fluency	Excellent comprehension Few grammatical errors
Advanced Fluency	Close to native speech

Source: Krashen and Terrell, 1983.

 IMPLEMENTATION TIP

The grade-level team (including the teacher for ELL) discussed a variety of options based on their assessment shown in Exhibit 6.2. Here are additional items they discussed to help them decide on the implementation:

► **Interventions** may include time, such as duration and frequency (e.g., 20, 30, 45 minutes a day, two times a week, daily); environment (physical location, structure); personnel (teacher, specialist); and grouping (small 1:5 or 1:3, heterogeneous, homogenous). The higher the tier, the smaller the group and the formative assessment (two times a month, weekly, two times a week, daily). The higher the tier, the more frequent the need for assessment to monitor the student's progress. Remember, core Tier 1 provides the research-based instruction with differentiation as needed, based on the pre-assessed needs of the students from a highly qualified teacher during core instruction. Students in Tiers 2–3 require intensified intervention strategies and activities.

► **Strategies** shown are samples of the intentional adult actions that should have the greatest positive impact on student learning, such as the use of realia, modeling, demonstrations, visuals, and total physical response (TPR). Select the strategy based on the strengths, challenges, and inferences discussed during the meeting.

► **Activities** shown are the actions of the student, such as the use of drawings to represent some concepts.

NOTE: This is not intended to be an exhaustive list of possible activities and strategies for this area of content. Typically, there is not a dividing line between some of the tiers. It may be that the strategy or classroom activity will be appropriate for multiple tiers. In some cases, the time, intensity, and duration of a strategy may be modified to suit particular groups or individual students. Read the "How Does It Look" section to see which strategy, activity, and assessment was used by this particular team. Discuss other strategies that may be appropriate based on the scenario.

HOW DOES IT LOOK?

During social studies class, Ms. Duncan began to use gestures and realia during the lesson to express key vocabulary that described the workers in a neighborhood. Aimee's eyes lit up when she recognized the doctors and began to understand the words *doctor, postal worker, grocer,* and so on. Ms. Duncan showed pictures and also provided opportunities for the students to mimic gestures representing the movements of, for example, a postal worker delivering mail. Next, students were shown a model and were asked to cut and paste photos of community members and place them in the appropriate environments. Ms. Duncan continued reinforcement of the new vocabulary by providing dress-up costumes so the students could take on the roles of the postal worker, nurse, doctor, grocer, and so on, during their playtime activity. During the math lesson, the students counted and categorized the photos of the community members on a large matrix.

EXHIBIT 6.2 Sample K–2 Vocabulary

Sample Tiers	Strategies and Activities	Description
1, 2, 3	Provide realia	Use real objects and visuals such as photographs.
1, 2, 3	Model and demonstrate	Directions are given by pointing, gesturing, showing, and explaining.
1, 2, 3	Videos, DVDs, audiocassettes	Provide sensory input through visuals or auditory reinforcement.
1, 2, 3	Hands-on activities	Draw pictures, sequence stories, experiment, pantomime.
1, 2, 3	Create nonlinguistic representations	Use graphic representations, pictures, mental images, physical or technological models, kinesthetic activities.
1, 2, 3	Alternative teaching (preteaching activity)	Students will receive preteaching of key vocabulary to be introduced in the lesson. This activity should take 3–5 minutes. This may be done with students who require targeted or intensive intervention while the other students are working on a bell ringer/warm-up or review activity.
1, 2, 3	Additional direct instruction or guided practice	Students may receive a double or triple dose of direct instruction during flex time or station rotation 10–15 minutes, 2–3 times per week.
1, 2, 3	Total Physical Response	Students respond to commands that require physical movement.
Additional:		
Additional:		
Additional:		

Source: Hill and Flynn, 2008.

 HOW IS IT MONITORED?

The kindergarten teachers decided to create a checklist that would help them appropriately monitor the acquisition of various key vocabulary words. The team first categorized the list based on the expectations of the state standards and then separately listed the words. They decided to assess the students once a week as a group to see if they were responding to the interventions. The checklist would then be compared and analyzed in the team meeting on a weekly basis to see if some students required targeted or more intensive intervention strategies.

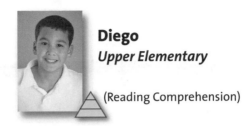

Diego
Upper Elementary

(Reading Comprehension)

Diego absolutely loves school. He moved to the United States with his parents, two brothers, and one sister a year ago. They are currently living with his uncle and his uncle's wife and two children. Diego's parents indicated that due to circumstances in his native Columbia, Diego was unable to attend school on a regular basis. He is very excited to be in school now and eagerly studies and actively participates in every activity.

Diego's parents are concerned about his progress in school and requested a conference with Mr. Haines, his fourth-grade general education teacher. During the conference, the parents asked if there were additional programs or services that Diego might receive to help boost his reading comprehension. They said they would be happy to help Diego at home if Mr. Haines could provide materials or information for more practice. Diego's father does speak some English, but his wife does not, so Spanish is spoken at home.

Fortunately, prior to the meeting with Diego's parents, Mr. Haines reviewed all of Diego's scores and documented his academic progress. Mr. Haines, along with the help of a translator, was able to discuss Diego's current level of performance and show the parents a graph of Diego's academic progress since the beginning of school in September up to the current date.

Mr. Haines explained that Diego appeared to be making good progress in his math classes. But comprehension in reading, social studies, and science was below proficient. Mr. Haines had hoped that using universal strategies at Tier 1 would be sufficient because Diego is such an eager learner and hard worker in class. But he now believes that Diego might indeed require more targeted intervention strategies to help him reach proficiency.

After a careful analysis of his work samples, the fourth-grade team determined that Diego should receive additional assistance in reading. He is making good progress in learning English but could use specific skill building. The team suggested that they begin with one intervention strategy for the next two weeks. In addition to the general teacher's direct instruction, the ELL teacher would work with four of the students in his class for an additional 30 minutes daily. Exhibit 6.3 lists a few of the intervention strategies discussed by the fourth-grade team.

Reflection: *Diego has just enrolled in your classroom. His language assessment indicates that he needs 30 minutes of supplemental reading comprehension instruction at least two to three times each week. You do not have an English Language Learner teacher available more than 30 minutes once each week. Now, what do you do? Justify your response.*

 IMPLEMENTATION TIP

The grade-level team discussed a variety of options based on their assessment shown in the exhibit below. Here are additional items they discussed to help them decide on the implementation:

▶ **Interventions** may include time, such as duration and frequency (e.g., 20, 30, 45 minutes a day, two times a week, daily); environment (physical location, structure); personnel (teacher, specialist); and grouping (small 1:5 or 1:3, heterogeneous, homogenous). The higher the tier, the smaller the group and the formative assessment (two times a month, weekly, two times a week, daily). The higher the tier, the more frequent the need for assessment to monitor the student's progress. Remember, core Tier 1 provides the research-based instruction with differentiation as needed, based on the pre-assessed needs of the students from a highly qualified teacher during core instruction. Students in Tiers 2–3 require intensified intervention strategies and activities.

▶ **Strategies** shown in the chart below are samples of the intentional adult actions that should have the greatest positive impact on student learning, such as the use of a comparison matrix or Venn Diagram (graphic organizer) to compare and contrast. Select the strategy based on the strengths, challenges, and inferences discussed during the meeting.

▶ **Activities** shown in the chart below are the actions of the student, such as the use of TPR to respond to key words or phrases prompted by the teacher.

NOTE: This is not intended to be an exhaustive list of possible activities and strategies for this area of content. Typically, there is not a dividing line between some of the tiers. It may be that the strategy or classroom activity will be appropriate for multiple tiers. In some cases, the time, intensity, and duration of a strategy may be modified to suit particular groups or individual students. Read the "How Does It Look" section to see which strategy, activity, and assessment was used by this particular team. Discuss other strategies that may be appropriate based on the scenario.

EXHIBIT 6.3	Sample Comprehension	
Sample Tiers	**Strategies and Activities**	**Description**
1, 2, 3	Direct instruction (explicit)	Double dose direct instruction in reading comprehension with general educator or push-in interventionist 15–30 minutes per day.
2, 3	ELL 30–60 minutes daily	Use direct instruction with ELL teacher daily for 30–60 minutes to supplement core instruction.
1, 2, 3	Cooperative learning	Students can work together in pairs, triads, or quads with a set of guidelines for cooperatively completing and sharing assignments.
1, 2, 3	Learning stations/centers	Provide reading activities for students to practice in a learning center (independent) or learning station (with guided instruction).
1, 2, 3	Nonlinguistic representations	Use graphic representations, pictures, mental images, physical or technological models, kinesthetic activities.
1, 2, 3	Compare and contrast familiar items	Compare and contrast items that are familiar along with the introduction of new items.
1, 2, 3	Graphic organizers (e.g., Venn or Comparison Matrix)	Provide guided practice in the use of graphic organizers. Provide models and ample time for demonstration and practice.
1, 2, 3	Model/demonstrate	Model, demonstrate, use body language, facial cues, visuals, hands-on manipulatives, realia, and total physical response.
Additional:		
Additional:		
Additional:		

Sources: Marzano, 2007; Hill and Flynn, 2008.

HOW DOES IT LOOK?

Mr. Haines began the new intervention strategies on the next school day (Monday). He first discussed a plan with the ELL teacher, Ms. Inouye. Ms. Inouye said that she would like to model and team teach some of the strategies with the entire class as well. She began immediately by demonstrating a lesson and showing the students how to respond with TPR. The students understood very quickly and found it quite engaging. Ms. Inouye felt confident that by working in the classroom with Diego and the three other students in small groups as well, Diego and his classmates would make good progress. Mr. Haines and Ms. Inouye agreed to evaluate their plan in two weeks during the regular team meeting. Mr. Haines typically uses station teaching or learning centers about two to three times a week. So he suggested that station teaching would be a good model that would maintain a normal flow in class during Ms. Inouye's targeted intervention.

 HOW IS IT MONITORED?

Ms. Inouye used the progress monitoring form (see Appendix G) to document Diego's progress. She shared the information with Mr. Haines following each session so that he could continue building the skills of similarities and differences with Diego. Ms. Inouye also was able to attend the bimonthly grade-level meeting on a monthly basis. She explained that due to her schedule split between two schools, monthly participation could work. She was grateful to know that the grade-level meeting notes could also be posted on the internal server. Mr. Haines continued his graph of the students' progress to see if they were responding as expected to the intervention and matching the goals set by the grade-level team. He felt confident that by using this method of monitoring every two weeks, any midcourse corrections could take place quickly before additional gaps developed in student achievement.

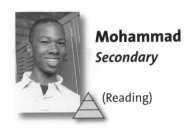

Mohammad
Secondary

(Reading)

Mohammad is originally from Nigeria, West Africa. He moved to the United States with his father two years ago. He speaks English but is most comfortable with his native language, Hausa, that is spoken at home. His hobbies include computer games, music, and sports, specifically soccer. Mohammad is slowly becoming accustomed to the American culture. He likes his mathematics and music classes best, but is struggling in his other academic courses. In each of the department meetings for social studies, science, and language arts, Mohammad's scores are discussed; they are significantly below proficient, although he is within a few points of proficiency in mathematics. While looking at his scores in reading and writing, one of the team members questioned whether he should be referred to the Student Teacher Assistance Team (STAT) for possible assessment for special education services. Several teachers in the department meeting agreed to the referral, including his science teacher, Ms. Tibbit. However, the department team leader wanted to first review the interventions that had been tried prior to a referral. Ms. Tibbit and the social studies teacher, Mr. Hubert, indicated that they provided more time for Mohammad to turn in assignments but truly did not attempt to differentiate the lessons or provide any other additional assistance. They thought perhaps he was simply unmotivated to complete his work appropriately or on time.

The team leader thought that on the surface this might seem to be a good strategy that might indeed work for most students but did not appear to meet the needs of Mohammad and perhaps a few other students on the class list. The team members agreed that they had skipped considering other intervention strategies that might provide targeted interventions for Mohammad and decided to pinpoint the problems and analyze his strengths, challenges, and the root causes of the problems rather than making the assumption that he was simply unmotivated. They agreed that targeted Tier 2 and Tier 3 interventions should be tried prior to referral to the STAT. What do you think of their decision?

The team decided to invite the ELL specialist to the next team meeting. They were shown Mohammad's language assessment scores and realized that although he speaks English, his native language (Hausa) is still his primary means of communication at home and in his community. Mohammad rarely asks questions in class, but he is frequently confused about the content or has difficulty following the teacher's directions. The ELL teacher said that his name slipped through the system, and he was never considered for additional language support. The team leader decided to request additional assessment to pinpoint his specific individual needs in reading. The assessments would begin immediately with another meeting to be held in two days. Mohammad is in ninth grade, and the team felt a sense of urgency to address the problem as quickly as possible. The leader further suggested that the team needed to complete their analysis, set goals, and begin the intervention strategies prior to the next meeting scheduled in two weeks. Exhibit 6.4 lists some of the instructional strategies and activities suggested based on the team's analysis for Mohammad and five other students experiencing similar academic problems in the department.

Reflection: *Based on the team members' discussion, do you believe that Mohammad should be referred now for special education testing? Why or why not? Justify your response.*

IMPLEMENTATION TIP

The English Department team (including the ELL teacher) discussed a variety of options based on their assessment shown in Exhibit 6.4. Here are additional items they discussed to help them decide on the implementation:

▶ **Interventions** may include time, such as duration and frequency (e.g., 20, 30, 45 minutes a day, two times a week, daily); environment (physical location, structure); personnel (teacher, specialist); and grouping (small 1:5 or 1:3, heterogeneous, homogenous). The higher the tier, the smaller the group and the formative assessment (two times a month, weekly, two times a week, daily). The higher the tier, the more frequent the need for assessment to monitor the student's progress. Remember, core Tier 1 provides the research-based instruction with differentiation as needed, based on the pre-assessed needs of the students from a highly qualified teacher during core instruction. Students in Tiers 2–3 require intensified intervention strategies and activities.

▶ **Strategies** shown are samples of the intentional adult actions that should have the greatest positive impact on student learning, such as the use of collaborative learning and nonlinguistic representations. Select the strategy based on the strengths, challenges, and inferences discussed during the meeting.

► **Activities** shown are the actions of the students, such as working in pairs or triads with a study partner with directions specific to the pre-assessed language acquisition level. Consider academic and social language levels of the students.

NOTE: This is not intended to be an exhaustive list of possible activities and strategies for this area of content. Typically, there is not a dividing line between some of the tiers. It may be that the strategy or classroom activity will be appropriate for multiple tiers. In some cases, the time, intensity, and duration of a strategy may be modified to suit particular groups or individual students. Read the "How Does It Look" section to see which strategy, activity, and assessment was used by this particular team. Discuss other strategies that may be appropriate based on the scenario.

 HOW DOES IT LOOK?

Each of Mohammad's core teachers decided to use the same intervention for two weeks. Each class used more visuals, realia, and cooperative learning. Teachers made a point of modeling and demonstrating key concepts on a daily basis and checking for understanding by asking for a thumbs up, nod, raised hand, or a short entrance slip. Mohammad's teachers also circulated around the room more, monitoring throughout the lesson rather than remaining at the front of the class. These were the first steps taken after analyzing the assessments and work samples shown to the team.

The team members also asked the ELL specialist to return to the next meeting and model additional strategies that could be used to help Mohammad and several other students interact at the appropriate levels in understanding grammar and pronunciation errors. Mohammad misunderstands jokes and many colloquial expressions, but when translated by a classmate into Hausa, he thoroughly enjoys the humor.

The core teachers also decided that it would be beneficial to provide alternative instruction for vocabulary with an advance organizer of (prewritten) Cornell Notes so that Mohammad could concentrate on the content and not be consumed with laboriously taking notes when he was still trying to understand the words. He could take notes alongside the preprinted prompts as needed.

After reviewing his initial Home Language Survey and the results of his initial language assessment and current scores, it was decided that the ELL teacher meet with Mohammad and four other classmates daily with a focus on text, fluency, and comprehension.

EXHIBIT 6.4

Sample Ninth-Grade Reading

Sample Tiers	Strategies and Activities	Description
1, 2, 3	Direct instruction (explicit)	A continuum of effective research-based strategies for increasing opportunities for learning by highly qualified teachers in the general education environment.
1, 2, 3	Study buddy/partner	At the beginning of class students are paired with a homogenous or heterogeneous partner that they can study with during class. During this time the students will share and discuss their notes with each other as the teacher monitors their work. (This is not the electronic Study Buddy product.)
1, 2, 3	Cooperative learning	Students work in cooperative homogeneous or heterogeneous pairs, triads, quads with set responsibilities for completing assignments or sharing information.
2, 3	Interactive journal	Students use a composition book to write their feelings, experiences, or responses to prompts. In this case the student kept a journal of his responses to the nonfiction books that he read each week.
2, 3	Nonlinguistic representations	Graphic representations, pictures, mental images, physical or technological models, kinesthetic activities.
2, 3	Alternative teaching	Students requiring targeted or intensive instruction may be gathered in a small group prior to the class lesson to discuss new vocabulary or preview concepts for 3–4 minutes. The remainder of the class may complete an entrance slip or bell ringer/warm-up activity.
2, 3	Graphic organizers (Cornell Notes and Comparison Matrix)	There are numerous advance organizers (such as Cornell Notes, or double-entry journals) to help students focus and organize information. Once students have learned the method of organizing information, they can make their own organizers as well. A large variety of graphic organizers are available online.
Additional:		
Additional:		
Additional:		

Sources: Marzano, 2007; Hill and Flynn, 2008.

HOW IS IT MONITORED?

Each of Mohammad's teachers agreed to individually implement the discussed interventions with fidelity and to maintain documentation on the progress monitoring form by keeping assessment notes and anecdotal records. The team leader asked the teachers to bring their progress monitoring notes to the meeting on a bimonthly basis and to be prepared to share their findings with the team. The team followed the same process of analyzing the current data and reviewing previous data for patterns and trends in performance. The team agreed to continue this procedure for the next eight weeks. The team also committed to providing short probative assessments to the students and to remaining poised to make midcourse corrections as needed.

HOW HAVE YOU THOUGHT ABOUT?

English language learners come to school with knowledge, skill, and a desire to learn more than the English language. Their experiences and background from their own culture provide educators with unique opportunities to involve these students in multiple ways in the classroom. Most ELL students will have the ability to understand and use oral language in routines, play, and social communication before they develop the use of written English. These students will need multiple learning experiences to listen, read, write, and speak across all curriculum areas.

As you reflect on the three students in the ELL scenarios, think about how their situation applies to your teaching and learning. Consider these questions:

► What learning barriers do you see in your ELLs? What best practices in reading and writing have you researched to use within your classroom?

► How do you collaborate with additional support teachers who work with the ELL students?

► How can you use additional teaching strategies (i.e., music, visual, kinesthetic) to enrich the learning experiences for your ELL students?

Appendices

APPENDIX A
Glossary

Behavior Intervention Plan

A plan for student behavior based on a Functional Behavior Assessment (FBA). The plan is a collaborative document that involves the teacher, student, parent, and anyone who has educational contact with the student.

Comparison Matrix

A graphic organizer that students can use to help them compare and contrast, analyze, evaluate, and synthesize multiple characteristics from a small to large list of items placed on the axis of the grid.

Cornell Notes

The Cornell note-taking method helps students organize their notes on a lined sheet of notebook paper in two columns. The column on the left is approximately two inches wide. This column is used for key words or phrases. The column on the right is for additional information or detail about the key word. The key words on the left can be used as "flash cards" if the paper is folded vertically to expose the left column only. At the bottom of the page, a brief summary of the page can be included as a study aid as well.

Differentiated Instruction (DI)

The process of designing lesson plans that meet the needs of the entire range of learners in the classroom. Such planning includes learning objectives, grouping practices, teaching methods, varied assignments, and varied materials chosen based on student skill levels, interest levels, and learning preferences.

English Language Learner (ELL)

A student whose home language is not English and who has not attained proficiency in English as measured by standardized tests.

Fidelity

Fidelity refers to the accuracy, loyalty, and attentiveness with which an intended research design for instruction and/or intervention is implemented. To ensure standardization, intervention specialists must generally follow a prescribed protocol in order to attend to a program's or strategy's fidelity.

Gap Analysis

Gap analysis is a tool for measuring the difference between a student's current level of performance and benchmark expectations.

Intervention

Systematic and explicit instruction provided to accelerate growth in an area of identified need. Interventions are provided by both special and general educators and are based on the educator's training. The interventions are designed to improve performance relative to specific and measurable goals. Interventions are based on valid information about current performance and a realistic implementation plan, and include ongoing student progress monitoring.

Multitiered Model

Providing differing levels of intensity, universal (Tier 1), targeted (Tier 2), or intensive (Tier 3), based on a student's responsiveness to intervention, with ongoing progress monitoring and focused assessment.

Problem-Solving Process

The problem-solving process is an interdisciplinary, collaborative team process that is based on a multitiered model and includes data-driven decision making, parent/school partnerships, progress monitoring, focused assessment, flexible service delivery, and prescriptive, research-based interventions.

Progress Monitoring

Progress monitoring is an ongoing process that requires the collection and analysis of data in order to determine student progress toward specific skills or general outcomes. Instructional decisions are also made based on the review and analysis of this data.

Scientifically Research-Based Interventions

A research-based instructional practice or intervention is one found to be reliable, trustworthy, and valid based on evidence suggesting that when the program is used with a particular group of children, the children can be expected to make adequate gains in achievement. Ongoing documentation and analysis of student outcomes help to define effective practice. In the absence of evidence, the instruction/intervention must be considered "best practice" based on available research and the professional literature.

Screening

A quick checklist, survey, or probe about a student's content development or skills to determine if further evaluation is needed.

Tier 1 (Universal) Intervention

Tier 1 instructional interventions are provided to all students in the classroom, typically through differentiated research-based instruction provided by the highly qualified classroom teacher.

Tier 2 (Targeted) Intervention

Tier 2 interventions are implemented when multiple probative student assessments indicate that the student is not making adequate gains from universal instruction alone.

Tier 3 (Intensive) Intervention

Tier 3 interventions provide individualized, systematic, and explicit instruction in an area of assessed need and are indicated when multiple probative assessments show that the student is not making adequate gains from Tier 1 or Tier 2 instructional interventions. Tier 3 interventions should supplement (add to) the instruction, not supplant (replace) it.

APPENDIX B
Response to Intervention (RTI) Web Sites

Benchmark Education	www.benchmarkeducation.com An extensive collection of high-interest fiction and nonfiction standards-aligned leveled texts, skill-building sets, and exceptional teacher tools are available for purchase.
Edcheckup	www.edcheckup.com Edcheckup™ offers a progress monitoring system for students in grades K–8 that evaluates student performance and measures student progress toward goals in reading, writing, and math.
EdProgress	www.edprogress.com EdProgress specializes in creating data integrated web based and stand alone applications and focuses on assessment, large-scale testing and accountability, and systemic reform.
LD Online	http://www.ldonline.Org An abundance of information and resources to support understanding of Response to Intervention (RTI).
The Iris Center	http://iris.peabody.vanderbilt.edu/index.html The IRIS Center provides free online interactive resources that translate research about the education of students with disabilities into practice. Their materials cover a wide variety of evidence-based topics, including behavior, RTI, learning strategies, and progress monitoring.
CTB McGraw-Hill Yearly Progress Pro	www.mhdigitallearning.com Yearly ProgressPro™ is web-based research-based assessment, instructional, and intervention tool that provides automatic intervention to ensure instruction is aligned to state and national standards.
National Association of State Directors of Special Education, Inc. (NASDSE)	http://www.nasdse.org This is the Web site for the National Association of State Directors of Special Education (NASDSE). NASDSE has been providing leadership to improve educational services and outcomes for students with disabilities throughout the United States.

pro*ed – an International Publisher	**www.proedinc.com** PRO-ED Inc. is a leading publisher of standardized tests, books, curricular resources, and therapy materials.
International Reading Association	**www.reading.org** The International Reading Association's Web site. This association supports literacy professionals through a wide range of resources, advocacy efforts, volunteerism, and professional development activities.
National Center on Response to Intervention	**www.rti4success.org** This site has a wealth of information related to response to intervention including tools/interventions, a library of resources, and training modules.
RTI Action Network	**http://www.rtinetwork.org** Contains a wealth of information geared to understanding and implementing RTI.
Rubistar.com	**www.rubistar.com** A resource for rubrics and performance assessment.
National Center on Student Progress Monitoring	**www.studentprogress.org** A Web site devoted to progress monitoring—a scientifically based practice that is used to assess students' academic performance and evaluate the effectiveness of instruction.
Literacy and Information Communication System (LINCS)	**http://lincs.ed.gov** The Literacy Information and Communication System (LINCS) is a national dissemination, resource gathering, and professional development system providing information on a wide variety of literacy-relevant topics, issues, and resources.

APPENDIX C
Bloom's Taxonomy Categories in the Cognitive Process Dimension

Most educators are quite familiar with Benjamin Bloom's *Taxonomy of Educational Objectives* (1956). For many, understanding the levels of thinking represented in this taxonomy was a cornerstone of required educational methods courses.

In recent years, as educators have become increasingly focused on the accurate assessment of student learning, the original taxonomy has been revisited and revised. Unlike the original, the revised framework is two-dimensional. In the newer model, the two dimensions are cognitive process and knowledge. These two components operate like the x and y axes in a graph: the cognitive level (evident from a verb that represents student learning) would be placed on the horizontal axis, and the type of knowledge (evident from the nouns that represent what the student is to learn) would be placed on the vertical axis.

The six cognitive processes in the revised taxonomy are to *remember, understand, apply, analyze, evaluate,* and *create.* These are just slightly different from the original six levels of Bloom's taxonomy. The four categories of knowledge in the revised taxonomy are *factual, conceptual, procedural,* and *metacognitive.*

This revised taxonomy works well with the "unwrapping" process and, later, in designing effective assessment items. In order to place an objective in the taxonomy, teachers must first "unwrap" a standard to discover what it requires cognitively (the verb) and in terms of knowledge (the nouns that delineate content and concepts). Once the correct placement is determined, the "bare bones" of the assessment items are set. However, the placement is important because different types of objectives require different approaches to assessment (Anderson and Krathwohl, 2000, p.8).

The following discussions of the six cognitive levels contain lists of verbs that approximate the particular levels of student learning. It is important to "unwrap" standards and ensure each standard is placed in the taxonomy table before designing appropriate assessment items.

Cognitive process 1: To *remember*
"To remember is to retrieve relevant knowledge from long-term memory"
(Anderson and Krathwohl, 2000, p. 67). Verbs associated with this level: choose,

define, describe, find, identify, label, list, locate, match, name, recall, recite, recognize, record, relate, retrieve, say, select, show, sort, and tell.

Cognitive process 2: To *understand*

"To understand is to construct meaning from instructional messages, including oral, written, and graphic communication" (Anderson and Krathwohl, 2000, p. 67). Verbs associated with this level: categorize, clarify, classify, compare, conclude, construct, contrast, demonstrate, distinguish, explain, illustrate, interpret, match, paraphrase, predict, reorganize, represent, summarize, translate, and understand.

Cognitive process 3: To *apply*

"To apply is to carry out or use a procedure in a given situation" (Anderson and Krathwohl, 2000, p. 67). Verbs associated with this level: apply, carry out, construct, develop, display, execute, illustrate, implement, model, solve, and use.

Cognitive process 4: To *analyze*

"To analyze is to break material into its constituent parts and determine how the parts relate to one another and to an overall structure or purpose" (Anderson and Krathwohl, 2000, p. 68). Verbs associated with this level: analyze, ascertain, attribute, connect, deconstruct, determine, differentiate, discriminate, dissect, distinguish, divide, examine, experiment, focus, infer, inspect, integrate, investigate, organize, outline, reduce, and solve (a problem).

Cognitive process 5: To *evaluate*

"To evaluate is to make judgments based on criteria and standards" (Anderson and Krathwohl, 2000, p. 68). Verbs associated with this level: appraise, assess, award, check, conclude, convince, coordinate, criticize, critique, defend, detect, discriminate, evaluate, judge, justify, monitor, prioritize, rank, recommend, support, test, and value.

Cognitive process 6: To *create*

"To create is to put elements together to form a coherent or functional whole; reorganize elements into a new pattern or structure; inventing a product" (Anderson and Krathwohl, 2000, p. 68). Verbs associated with this level: adapt, build, compose, construct, create, design, develop, elaborate, extend, formulate, generate, hypothesize, invent, make, modify, plan, produce, originate, refine, and transform.

APPENDIX D
Sample Universal Screening Instruments

Early Education	Dynamic Indicators of Basic Early Literacy Skills (DIBELS)	http://dibels.uoregon.edu
	Kindergarten Curriculum-Based Measurement (K-CBM)	http://www.gosbr.net/screening
	Phonological Awareness Literacy Screening (PALS)	http://pals.virginia.edu
Reading	AIMSweb	www.aimsweb.com/measures/reading/sample.php
	Northwest Evaluation Association (NWEA)	www.nwea.org
	Read Naturally	www.readnaturally.com/howto/
	Pearson Prosper	www.pearsonncs.com
	Pearson Benchmark	www.pearsonschoolsystems.com
	Riverside Assess2Know	www.riverpub.com/products/a2k/
	Developmental Reading Assessment (DRA)	www.pearsonschool.com
	Learning Access!	www.vantagelearning.com
	CTB McGraw-Hill	www.ctb.com
	Renaissance Learning	www.renlearn.com
	STAR Reading, Math, and Early Literacy	http://www.renlearn.com/sel/
Mathematics	AIMSweb	http://www.aimsweb.com/measures/math/sample.php
	Northwest Evaluation Association (NWEA)	www.nwea.org
	Pearson Benchmark	www.pearsonschoolsystems.com
	Riverside Assess2Know	www.riverpub.com/products/a2k/
	Learning Access!	www.vantagelearning.com
Curriculum	Curriculum Based-Measures	http://www.education.umn.edu/Pubs/ResearchWorks/CBM.html
		www.easycbm.com
		http://www.interventioncentral.org/

APPENDIX E
Team Meeting Forms

RTI Sample Interventionists

Possible interventionists	List personnel available in your school for RTI
General Education Teacher	
Special Education Teacher	
Instructional Coach	
Occupational Therapist	
Speech and Language Pathologist	
School Counselor	
Parent	
Social Worker	
Paraprofessional	
School Psychologist	
University Tutors	
Community Volunteers (organizations)	
University Student Teachers	

APPENDIX E
Team Meeting Forms (continued)

Team Meeting Minutes

Power Standard:	
Success Criteria:	
Today's Date:	Date of Next Meeting:

Team Members Present:
Team Leader:
Note Taker:
Data Technician:
Time Keeper/Focus Monitor:
Active Participants:

Data Sources:

Students Below Proficient:	Students Close to Proficient:
Students Proficient:	Students Above Proficient:

Smart Goal:	Responsible for Progress Monitoring:
Percentage of _____ proficient and higher in specific standard will increase from _____ to _____ by _____ as measured by _____ given on _____.	Targeted Scientifically Research-Based Interventions:

Evaluation of the Response to the Above Interventions:

Have interventions been implemented with fidelity?
☐ Not implemented ☐ Partially implemented ☐ Fully implemented

Student achievement results:

Success indicators (evidence of actual impact on student learning):

Reasons why interventions were or were not successful:

Suggested adjustments or recommendations:

Adapted from Englewood School District, Colorado

APPENDIX E
Team Meeting Forms (continued)

Formative Assessment Form

Teacher: _____

School: _____ Grade: _____ Date of assessment: _____

Assessment name: _____

Proficient _____ Close to Proficient _____ Significantly below Proficiency_____

Students	Reading	Writing	Math	Performance notes

APPENDIX F

RTI Implementation Plan

Implement	Current state: Where we are	Plan of action: How will we implement it?	Desired state: Where we want to be
Communicate expectations			
Form collaborative teams			
Schedule collaborative meetings			
Conduct or review universal screening			
Review district resources			
Determine student tiers			

Implement 5-Step RTI Process:	Current state: Where we are	Plan of action: How will we implement it?	Desired state: Where we want to be
Complete Step 1			
Complete Step 2			
Complete Step 3			
Complete Step 4			
Complete Step 5			
External communication			
Additional notes:			

APPENDIX G

Progress Monitoring Form

Progress Monitoring Report
Response to Intervention

Initial date: _____

Name of student: _____ Birth date: _____ Age: _____

Specify target or intensive group: _____

List names:

School: _____

District: _____ Grade: _____

City: _____ State: _____

Progress Monitor: _____

Position: _____

1. What is the problem? (Assessment/date):

2. Which research-based intervention will be monitored? (Based on team analysis):

3. Which method(s) and what frequency will be used to progress monitor?

☐ Assessment scores: _____
   (Name/results/dates)

☐ Administrative walk-through/sweeps: _____
   (Dates and times)

☐ Observations: _____
   (Frequency/class/dates/time)

☐ Interviews: _____
   (Name[s])

☐ Data Team/PLC: _____
   (Date/results)

Universal screening results (Fall): _____

Universal screening results (Winter): _____

Universal screening results (Spring): _____

Behavior notes:

APPENDIX G
Progress Monitoring Form (continued)

Student/Group _____

Progress monitoring data:

Baseline   Intervention

Baseline results:

Monitoring intervals: ☐ Daily ☐ Biweekly ☐ Weekly ☐ Bimonthly ☐ Monthly

Ref. #	Monitoring narrative (date/results):	Determine effectiveness or need for further change in intensity, time, or resources (date/results):

APPENDIX G
Progress Monitoring Form (continued)

Progress Monitoring Team Analysis

Student(s):

Problem statement:	
Strengths:	Inferences:
Challenge/Weakness:	Inferences:

Root cause:

All interventions must be provided with fidelity.

Tier 1	Universal	Provide high-quality scientifically research-based instruction and differentiation of content, process, or product in general education. This applies to all students based on their individual needs.
Tier 2	Targeted	General education instruction of Tier 1 plus specialized intervention that includes consideration of small group, specific minutes per day or week lasting approximately 30 minutes each session.
Tier 3	Intensive	Students who did not respond to Tier 2 interventions require intensive instruction that includes increased frequency, duration, and smaller groups, sometimes 1:1.

APPENDIX H
RTI Interventions

QUICK REFERENCE OF SAMPLE INTERVENTION STRATEGIES

The strategies that follow are not meant to be a checklist of interventions. Nor is this to be considered an exhaustive or one-size-fits-all list of interventions. Additionally, the reader may find that there can indeed be a crossover in grades or in tiers. Please remember that it is necessary to collect appropriate data, to carefully analyze the strengths of and challenges for the student, as well as to determine the root causes of the issues that you are working with to assist the student.

Sample Tier 1 Interventions

All students must receive high-quality, evidence-based classroom instruction. Tier 1 instruction must be implemented with fidelity and appropriately progress monitored to determine the students' responses to intervention. The school must also use high-quality core curriculum.

- Differentiate instruction (content, process, product)
- Additional instructional time
- Change of environment or venue
- Assistive technology
- Graphic organizers
- Pre/re-teach/alternative instruction
- Change pace
- Repetition
- Systematic sequential instruction
- Modified curriculum
- Manipulatives
- Collaborative learning activities
- Direct/explicit instruction
- Chunking
- Address learning modalities (i.e., visual, auditory, kinesthetic, tactical, olfactory, and gustatory)
- Accommodate learning-style preferences

130

- Provide additional guided practice
- Instructional strategies
- Similarities and differences
- Summarizing and note taking
- Feedback and recognition
- Relationship/rapport
- Homework and practice
- Nonlinguistic representations
- Setting objectives, providing feedback
- Generating and testing hypotheses
- Cueing and signaling
- Appropriate questioning and response skills
- Advance organizers

Sample Tier 2 Interventions

For those students who do not make appropriate progress from the Tier 1 instruction, the problem-solving team may also develop targeted Tier 2 interventions. Before moving to Tier 2, make sure to take multiple assessment probes of student achievement and consider adjustments of frequency, duration, and intensity of Tier 1 strategies. Again, it is assumed that Tier 1 interventions were conducted with fidelity within the appropriate core curriculum and with adequate progress monitoring.

Evaluate student responses to Tier 1 interventions and then:

- Increase intervention frequency, intensity, and duration of instruction
- Include social worker, reading specialist/coach, math specialist/coach
- Supplement the curriculum
- Double-dose the instruction
- Add before- or after-school tutorial program
- Add adult or student mentor
- Add computer-assisted instruction or device (e.g., AlphaSmart)
- Add study-skills class
- Add study buddy or tutorials
- Add special-skills class
- Hold a parent conference
- Alter class schedule (if possible)
- Set up a homework hotline

- Add video instruction
- Add accelerated courses
- Add computerized (content) programs
- Add advance organizers
- Add cross-class courses
- Conduct a task analysis
- Add enhanced tutorials
- Use a more rigorous curriculum

Sample Tier 3 Interventions

If a student does not make the expected academic progress after the implementation of Tiers 1 and 2, the grade-level or department team should carefully review and analyze the data to provide intensive interventions for the student. Before moving to Tier 3, make sure to take multiple assessment probes of student achievement and consider adjustments of frequency, duration, and intensity of Tier 2 intervention strategies. Remember that Tiers 2 and 3 should not supplant the direct instruction of the classroom teacher provided with fidelity at Tier 1. Rather, Tiers 2 and 3 should supplement the instruction of the teacher by providing additional resources for intensive instruction to help the student.

Evaluate student responses to Tier 1 and Tier 2 interventions and then:

- Increase intervention frequency, intensity, and duration
- Add intensive core adult support
- Add intensive learning plan
- Add individual behavior plan (assessment, contract, reinforcement, and modeling)
- Include occupational therapist, speech and language pathologist, paraprofessional, school psychologists, social workers
- Modify cooperative group
- Add individualized intervention
- Triple-dose the instruction
- Increase opportunities to use learning-style preferences
- Evaluate teaching style
- Increase the use of sensory modalities
- Provide individual differentiated content, process, and product
- Evaluate and modify learning environment
- Develop a Focus Support Program (FSP), individual or small-group pull-out, or resource program for intensive incremental skills

TIER 1 INTERVENTIONS

Sample K–2 Writing Intervention Strategies

Sample Tiers	Intervention Strategies	To be Conducted by the General Education Teacher/Interventionist in Class*
1, 2, 3	Provide proper writing instruments	Provide appropriate size and thickness of the writing instrument. A pencil grasp may also be used.
1,2,3	Provide ample time	Time should be available as an advance lesson (bell ringer) prior to the lesson, immediately following the class activity, or during a designated additional time, for example, 5–10 minutes of additional direct instruction and independent practice.
2,3	Trace over paper or on top of model letters	Student should lightly trace on top of preprinted letters on paper. Focus on the letters the student does not form correctly. Practice the correct form of one or more letters each day.
2,3	Trace over tactile surface	Trace letters on fine sandpaper, felt cutouts, shaving cream, or other tactile surface with finger and then with a pencil.
3	Trace on the student's back	Trace a letter with your finger (e.g., the letter K) on the student's back as you say the letter. Ask them to repeat the letter.
3	Trace in clay	Trace letters on soft clay with finger.
3	Use raised lines on paper	Paper with raised lines is commonly used for students with visual impairments as well. Use color-coded and start-stop symbol paper for primary grades.
2,3	Contrast colors on text or background	Use light-colored paper—pale pink, yellow, green, beige, etc.
2,3	Provide additional supervised practice	Provide direct supervised (one-on-one to one-on-three) observation of student practice. If necessary add a sheet of very fine sandpaper under the writing sheet to help with writing control.
2,3	Learning center/Learning stations	Provide writing prompts, tracing sheets, and ample opportunity for students to practice in a learning center (independent) or learning station (guided).
Additional:		
Additional:		
Additional:		

* Note: In most cases the general education teacher may provide the intervention/strategy described in the right-hand column. Additional interventionists may be available at the school to assist the teacher as needed.

Intervention strategies may vary. For example, Tier 2 intervention may be appropriate for a student in Tier 1 or 3, or a Tier 3 intervention strategy may be appropriate for Tier 2 as well. The decision about which strategy to use and it's time, duration, and frequency must be based on the analysis of the student's needs.

Interventionists may include, but are not limited to, instructional coaches, literacy specialists, special education specialists, English Language Learner (ELL) specialists, paraprofessionals, training community volunteers such as from the Core of Retired Teachers, university students, related services personnel such as occupational/physical therapists, speech and language pathologists, and counselors or social workers. There are districts that describe this approach as "all hands on deck" to help the students. There have been individual discussions in school districts to determine who is qualified to provide the interventions. Typically, the licensed or certified professional should provide the direct instruction and all others may provide the continued guided practice and content and skill development.

Source: House (2004)

TIER 1 INTERVENTIONS *(continued)*

Sample Spelling Intervention Strategies

Sample Tiers	Intervention Strategies	To be Conducted by the General Education Teacher in Class
1, 2, 3	Graphic organizer	Dissect the word, i.e., root word, part of speech, syllables for key words.
2, 3	Highlight root words	Underline root words in pencil or highlighter.
1, 2, 3	Explicit spelling rules	Consistently practice a spelling rule, such as "*i* before *e* except after *c*." Practice prefix and suffix, etc. Post-assess. When a rule is mastered, a new one is introduced.
1, 2, 3	Devlop a spelling thesaurus	When a new topic is introduced, students can create a visual thesaurus. See Exhibit 1.6.
1, 2, 3	Entrance/exit slip	Students can use a few minutes of class responding to a very short assessment of the spelling words every two days or once a week.
1, 2, 3	Physical practice (repetition)	Some students need to write the words several times.
2, 3	Mnemonics	Mnemonic rhymes, phrases, and illustrations that assist in remembering.
Additional:		
Additional:		
Additional:		

Sources: House, 2004; Marzano, 2007

TIER 2 INTERVENTIONS

Sample Number Sense Intervention Strategies

Sample Tiers	Intervention Strategies	To be Conducted by the General Education Teacher in Class
1, 2, 3	Tactile counters	Use counting blocks or tangible manipulatives that students can move around in various groups.
2, 3	Extend guided practice	Give students more time and multiple opportunities to interact with the numbers in a variety of settings so that they will recognize the similarities and relationship of numbers to context.
2, 3	Color code patterned numbers	Numbers may be color coded by patterns such as multiples of twos, threes, etc.
2, 3	Kinesthetic activity	Allow students to, for example, hop as they count, stretch and pretend to be numbers, hold up number cards, and move around to manipulate the cards in order and in patterned groups.
Additional:		
Additional:		
Additional:		

Source: Stein, Silbert, and Carnine, 1997.

TIER 2 INTERVENTIONS *(continued)*

Sample Mathematics Intervention Strategies

Sample Tiers	Intervention Strategies	To be Conducted by the General Education Teacher in Class
1, 2, 3	Alternative preteaching	Students requiring targeted or intensive instruction may be gathered in a small group prior to the class lesson for 3–4 minutes to discuss new math vocabulary, review problem solving. The remainder of the class may complete an entrance slip or bell ringer/warm-up activity.
2, 3	Direct instruction	A continuum of effective research-based strategies for increasing opportunities for learning by highly qualified teachers in the general education environment.
2, 3	Station teaching	Students rotate in small groups to a variety of learning stations, including one that includes direct instruction from the teacher.
2, 3	Tutoring	Tutoring may be presented before, during, or after school. The team should determine the time, duration, and intensity of the tutoring. It should be a second or third dose to supplement the core instruction.
1, 2, 3	Double entry journal	In this example, the student will write the mathematics problem in the left column or page and solve the problem in digits and words or nonlinguistic representations.
1, 2, 3	Computerized math programs	Research-based computerized math programs are available at the What Works Clearinghouse at http://ies.ed.gov/ncee/wwc/
2, 3	Additional guided practice time	Additional guided practice time may last 7–15 minutes. or 15–30 minutes based on student need. This can be done before or after class, during station rotation, flex time, or with a push-in interventionist during class.
Additional:		
Additional:		
Additional:		

Source: U.S. Department of Education, Institute of Education Sciences. What Works Clearinghouse at http://ies.ed.gov/ncee/wwc/

TIER 2 INTERVENTIONS *(continued)*

Sample Mathematics Skills Intervention Strategies*

Sample Tiers	Intervention Strategies	To be Conducted by the General Education Teacher
2, 3	Math coach or university volunteer tutor 20 minutes 2–3 times a week	A math coach, tutor, retired teacher or other interventionist can push-in or pull-out a small group of students in Tier 2. Push-in can be accomplished with learning stations or during cooperative learning groups.
2, 3	Advance organizers	Students are provided with an organizer in advance of the lesson that explicitly highlights the problem-solving steps.
1, 2, 3	Math strategies notebook	Provide explicit instruction on this graphic organizer. Students are to write each new mathematics problem on the left side and fill in how it was solved on the right side of the graphic.
2, 3	Highlighted vocabulary	Vocabulary should be translated into the numerals or operations to be used for each section.
1, 2, 3	Step-by-step word problems	The teacher can provide in writing and through modeling and demonstrating in small sections a step-by-step process to solve problems. Remember to provide opportunity for inquiry.
2, 3	Additional practice time	Students in Tiers 2 and 3 are provided with additional time during class, e.g., during flex activities, warm-up, or independent practice.
2, 3	Tutorial	Targeted tutoring provided before, during, or after school. Interventionist to supplement not supplant instruction 15–30 minutes 1–5 times per week.
Additional:		
Additional:		
Additional:		

**Note: This is not meant as an exhaustive list of the instructional strategies, interventions, or activities.

Sources: Ainsworth and Christinson, 2006; Stein, Silbert, and Carnine, 1997; House, 2004.

TIER 3 INTERVENTIONS

Sample Phonemic Awareness Intervention Strategies*

Sample Tiers	Intervention Strategies	To be Conducted by the General Education Teacher, Volunteers
2, 3	Phoneme isolation	Students recognize individual sounds in a word. The teachers may use a variety of kinesthetic, tactile, auditory, and visual methods. These strategies were used successfully in each of the items shown in the remaining cells of this chart.
1, 2, 3	Phoneme identity	Students recognize the same sounds in different words.
1, 2, 3	Phoneme categorization	Students recognize the word in a set of three or four words that have the "odd" sound.
1, 2, 3	Phoneme blending	Students listen to a sequence of separately spoken phonemes and then combine the phonemes to form a word. Then they write and read the word.
1, 2, 3	Phoneme segmentation	Students break a word into its separate sounds, saying each sound as they tap out or count it. Then they write and read the word.
1, 2, 3	Phoneme deletion	Students recognize the word that remains when a phoneme is removed from another word.
1, 2, 3	Phoneme addition	Students make a new word by adding a phoneme to an existing word.
1, 2, 3	Phoneme substitution	Students substitute one phoneme for another to make a new word.
2, 3	Additional guided practice	Students were given an additional 15 minutes a day. The work time began with 3–5 minutes building to 15 minutes. The teacher kept note of their time on graph paper with a check mark next to minute increments.
2, 3	Tutorial	Students received supplemental assistance 15–20 minutes three times per week with either the classroom teacher or an interventionist. This was before, during (flex), or after school. During school it is at the discretion of the team but should not supplant direct core instruction.
3	Special education	Special education teacher worked directly with the students who required intensive intervention. Three of the 5 students had an Individualized Education Program (IEP) in reading. Specially Designed Instruction (SDI)** was used to assist students.
Additional:		
Additional:		
Additional:		

* Note: This is not meant as an exhaustive list of the instructional strategies, interventions, or activities.
** Specially Designed Instruction (SDI) takes into account the content skills, student strengths, and challenges as well as the disability in order to design instruction to meet the needs of individual students.

Source: Literacy and Information Communication System (LINCS) http://lincs.ed.gov

TIER 3 INTERVENTIONS *(continued)*

Sample Text Comprehension Intervention Strategies

Sample Tiers	Intervention Strategies	To be Conducted by the General Education Teacher, Volunteers, Retired Teachers, Special Education Teacher
2, 3	Extended time 45 minutes after school	Attend an after-school program to supplement core and targeted instruction in reading comprehension 2–3 times per week.
2, 3	Alternate instruction	Provide visual cues or mini-lesson in advance of core instruction.
2, 3	Monitoring comprehension	Identify where the difficulty occurs, identify what the difficulty is, restate the difficult sentence or passage in their own words. Look back through the text, look forward in the text for information that might help them to resolve the difficulty.
2, 3	Metacognition skill development	Learn to use metacognitive strategies to think about and have control over reading.
2, 3	Graphic and semantic organizers	Use graphic organizers such as maps, webs, graphs, charts, frames, or clusters to help focus on concepts and how they are related to other concepts and to visually represent information and help with organization.
2, 3	Answering questions	Instruct students to answer questions that require an understanding of information that is: • text explicit (stated explicitly in a single sentence), • text implicit (implied by information presented in two or more sentences), or • information not found in the text at all, but part of the reader's prior knowledge or experience.
2, 3	Generating questions	Teach students to ask themselves questions that require them to integrate information from different segments of text. For example, students can be taught to ask main-idea questions that relate to important information in a text.
2, 3	Recognizing story structure	Instruct students to identify the categories of content (setting, initiating events, internal reactions, goals, attempts, and outcomes) and how this content is organized into a plot. Graphic organizers such as story maps can be used to show the sequence of events and organization.
2, 3	Summarizing	Identify or generate main ideas, connect the main or central ideas, eliminate redundant and unnecessary information, and remember what was read.
	Special education	Participate in Specially Designed Instruction (SDI) from the special education teacher.
2, 3	Prior knowledge	As part of previewing, ask the students what they already know about the content of the selection. Ask them what they know about the author and what text structure he is likely to use. Discuss the important vocabulary used in the text. Show students some pictures or diagrams to prepare them for what they are about to read.
2, 3	Mental imagery	Help readers form mental pictures, or images, as they read. Make sure the vocabulary is clear and if necessary provide visual images so the students have a frame of reference for the mental imagery. (Google Images is a quick resource for finding pictures.)
Additional:		
Additional:		
Additional:		

Sources: Literacy and Information Communication System (LINCS) http://lincs.ed.gov
Marzano, 2001; Pierangelo, 2003.

TIER 3 INTERVENTIONS *(continued)*

Sample Writing Intervention Strategies

Sample Tiers	Intervention Strategies	To be Conducted by the General Education Teacher, Volunteers, Retired Teachers, Special Education Teacher
2, 3	Extended time 45 minutes after school	Offer students additional time twice each week for supplemental writing practice under the guidance of one of the English teachers. (Teachers can rotate their time as an interventionist with small groups of students.)
2, 3	Advance organizers	Demonstrate writing organizers and provide formats to students to help with organization of writing.
2, 3	Alternate instruction	Provide students with rubrics and exemplars in advance of the writing lesson.
2, 3	In-school tutorial 30 minutes, three times a week	Students receiving supplemental services in Tier 3 can meet with a member of the Core of Retired Teachers and university student volunteers to help supplement the core instruction of the general education teacher. This can be conducted on scheduled flex activity assignment days or during prearranged cooperative learning sections of class. The student's teacher or interventionist can monitor and keep records.
1, 2, 3	Entrance/Exit slips	Students are provided with either an entrance or an exit slip (short 1–3 questions or prompts) assessment daily. To save scoring time, students may quickly learn to score and chart many of their own slips.
3	Special education services two times a week for 45 minutes	Provide Specially Designed Instruction (SDI) for those students eligible for special education services.
2, 3	Parallel teaching	Classes may be split in half with two teachers using the same content but in some cases different processes or methods to help students with the lesson. This may be done to lower the overall class size of instruction or to create smaller, homogeneous groups of students for the lesson as needed.
2, 3	Team teaching	Both the general and special education teachers work together to provide writing lessons for all three tiers to address the needs of individual students.
Additional:		
Additional:		
Additional:		

Sources: Peery, 2010;
    Literacy and Information Communication System (LINCS) http://lincs.ed.gov
    U.S. Department of Education, Institute of Education Sciences, What Works Clearinghouse at http://ies.ed.gov/ncee/wwc/

SPECIAL EDUCATION INTERVENTIONS

Sample K–2 Sequencing Intervention Strategies*

Sample Tiers	Intervention Strategies	To be Conducted by the General Education Teacher
2, 3	Use manipulatives (cubes) while counting	
1, 2	Partner or peer buddy while counting	Pair student for a few minutes several times a week with a peer who has developed the sequencing skill already. It does not have to be the same peer each time.
3	Computer practice along with manipulatives	Use computer software for practice but include tangible (manipulative) practice with each screen.
2, 3	Repetition	Student should be prompted to verbally repeat the first and second directions required. Next, do the activity and repeat the direction. Ask student to verbalize to check for understanding before adding another step.
2, 3	Visual cues and prompts	Provide verbal modeling, pictures, or demonstrations during two- or three-step directions.
Additional:		
Additional:		

* Note: This is not meant as an exhaustive list of the instructional strategies, interventions, or activities.

Source: House, 2004

SPECIAL EDUCATION INTERVENTIONS *(continued)*

Sample Grades 4–6 Multiplication Facts and Division Intervention Strategies*

Sample Tiers	Intervention Strategies	To be Conducted by the General Education Teacher, Volunteers, Retired Teachers, Instructional Coach, Special Education Teacher
2, 3	Flash cards/visual practice with peers	Practice multiplication tables with a peer. Use as a homework assignment as well. Use the new fact (e.g., six) in numerous ways throughout the day. Pay special attention to having students notice the numbers and patterns whenever possible in their environment.
2, 3	www.IXL.com (computer program practice)	Opportunities for additional drill and practice outside of the general lesson online. There are numerous computerized software programs that may provide sustainable practice through interesting graphics and sequential applications.
2, 3	National Library of Visual Manipulatives http://nlvm.usu.edu/en/nav/vlibrary.html (online manipulatives)	This Web site may be reached through http://free.ed.gov as well. These manipulatives may be created as plastic cardstock. If the computer is used for additional drill and practice, make sure that it is being carefully monitored for accuracy and not just random selection. For example, periodically ask the student to justify their selection or to explain their procedures prior to pressing the enter key.
2, 3	Kinesthetic activity during PE class	Physical education, art, and music teachers can integrate mathematics into their lessons when possible. The core teacher should let them know the math facts or the unit that is being taught.
3	Thirty minutes, three times a week, with special education teacher (push-in)	The number of minutes of specially designed instruction provided by the special educator is designated by the IEP team members.
2, 3	Patterning exercises	Provide patterns on paper, in the room, or through exercises that allow students to see groups and patterns of objects and numbers. Relationships should be considered (e.g., Could this group of three blocks go into five? How many times?)
1, 2, 3	Create charts (exemplars)	Allow students to create charts of exemplars with their written explanations (student-friendly language) of how to solve the problem.
1, 2, 3	Math journal	Students maintain a journal of new problem-solving methods, e.g., how they in their own words solved the problem. Language experience approach can be used here for students who struggle with writing. In this strategy, the student dictates the information to a teacher, volunteer, paraprofessional, or interventionist for the journal.
Additional:		
Additional:		
Additional:		

* Note: This is not meant as an exhaustive list of the instructional strategies, interventions, or activities discussed by the team.

Source: Stein, Silbert, and Carnine, 1997.

SPECIAL EDUCATION INTERVENTIONS *(continued)*

Sample Ninth-Grade Reading Intervention Strategies

Sample Tiers	Intervention Strategies	To be Conducted by the General Education Teacher, Volunteers
3	Electronic reader (WYNN or Kurzweil)	Windows XP, WYNN Reader (Freedom Scientific), and Kurzweil are a few examples of content-activated readers that will assist students in hearing the text of their curriculum materials that have been scanned.
3	Camtasia (computer lessons)	Use recorded PowerPoint and computer lessons (sound and visuals).
2, 3	Vocabulary skill development (special education teacher)	Provide alternative teaching activities to front-load vocabulary using specially designed instruction with graphic organizers and preprinted lecture notes.
2, 3	Direct instruction	Provide explicit reading strategies with frequent assessment and monitoring within the context of the course content.
2, 3	Increased use of visuals and hands-on activities	Use social studies and science demonstrations, modeling, video clips (when possible), hands-on activities.
Additional:		
Additional:		
Additional:		

Source: House, 2004.

GIFTED AND TALENTED INTERVENTIONS

Sample K–12 Mathematics Intervention Strategies

Sample Tiers	Intervention Strategies	To be Conducted by the General Education Teacher, University Volunteers, Math Coach
2, 3	Flexible grouping	Students will be assigned to small collaborative homogeneous groups. The groups will change based on pre- and post-assessments.
2, 3	Pre- and post-assessments	In addition to the universal screening, a short formative assessment will be used on a weekly basis with observation of student performance between assessments.
1, 2, 3	Learning centers	Learning centers will provide opportunities for independent practice with inquiry-based activities.
1, 2, 3	Learning stations	Students will be able to move to 3–4 learning stations that will give them the opportunity not only to work together but also to rotate to targeted, differentiated direct instruction and guided practice.
2, 3	Specific materials	The teacher can use scientifically research-based instructional materials specifically designed for gifted and talented students.
Additional:		
Additional:		
Additional:		

Sources: The National Research Center on the Gifted and Talented (NRC/GT), University of Connecticut, http://www.gifted.uconn.edu/nrcgt.html; National Council of Teachers of Mathematics (NCTM), http://www.nctm.org/

GIFTED AND TALENTED INTERVENTIONS *(continued)*

Sample Fourth-Grade Writing Intervention Strategies

Sample Tiers	Intervention Strategies	To be Conducted by the General Education Teacher, Volunteers, Retired Teachers
2, 3	Maintain an interactive journal	Students use a composition book to write their feelings, experiences, or responses to prompts. In this case, the student kept a journal of his responses to the nonfiction books that he read each week.
2, 3	Develop a cross-classroom, school, district, state, country, or world pen pal	Students may use letter writing, e-mail, or blogs to communicate with pen pals on a variety of topics.
1, 2, 3	Provide an opportunity to share materials	Student clubs are formed around writing interests as a forum to share their writing; for example, poetry clubs, short story clubs, clubs for writing plays. Ultimately work can be selected for publication in the local school or community newspaper.
Additional:		
Additional:		
Additional:		

Source: Literacy and Information Communication System (LINCS) http://lincs.ed.gov

GIFTED AND TALENTED INTERVENTIONS *(continued)*

Sample Ninth-Grade Mathematics Intervention Strategies

Sample Tiers	Intervention Strategies	To be Conducted by the General Education Teacher, Volunteers, Retired Teachers
1, 2, 3	Homogeneous cooperative groups	Use similar-strength pairs, triads, or quads; jigsaw.
1, 2, 3	Individual menu selection	Provide a list of process skill activities at different levels and a list of products that students can select from at least 2–3 times a month. Performance products will require a rubric as well. Once students are provided with an exemplar and the standards, they can write rubrics for approval.
1, 2, 3	Self-selection for group	Students can decide which configuration of study partners they prefer.
2, 3	Accelerated classes	Students can attend advanced placement classes, Gifted and Talented (GT) courses, community college courses, or supervised online classes.
Additional:		
Additional:		
Additional:		

Sources: Marzano, 2007;
        Literacy and Information Communication System (LINCS) http://lincs.ed.gov

ENGLISH LANGUAGE LEARNER INTERVENTIONS

Sample K–2 Vocabulary Intervention Strategies

Sample Tiers	Intervention Strategies	To be Conducted by the General Education Teacher, Volunteers, Retired Teachers
1, 2, 3	Provide realia	Use real objects and visuals such as photographs.
1, 2, 3	Model and demonstrate	Directions are given by pointing, gesturing, showing, and explaining.
1, 2, 3	Videos, DVDs, audiocassettes	Provide sensory input through visuals or auditory reinforcement.
1, 2, 3	Hands-on activities	Draw pictures, sequence stories, experiment, pantomime.
1, 2, 3	Create nonlinguistic representations	Use graphic representations, pictures, mental images, physical or technological models, kinesthetic activities.
1, 2, 3	Alternative teaching (preteaching activity)	Students receive preteaching of key vocabulary to be introduced in the lesson. This activity should take 3–5 minutes. This may be done with students who require targeted or intensive intervention while the other students are working on a bell ringer/warm-up or review activity.
1, 2, 3	Additional direct instruction or guided practice	Students may receive a double or triple dose of direct instruction during flex time or station rotation 10–15 minutes, 2–3 times per week.
Additional:		
Additional:		
Additional:		

Source: Hill and Flynn, 2008.

ENGLISH LANGUAGE LEARNER INTERVENTIONS *(continued)*

Sample Comprehension Intervention Strategies

Sample Tiers	Intervention Strategies	To be Conducted by the General Education Teacher, Volunteers, Retired Teachers
1, 2, 3	Direct instruction (explicit)	Double dose direct instruction in reading comprehension with general educator or push-in interventionist 15–30 minutes per day.
2, 3	ELL 30–60 minutes daily	Use direct instruction with ELL teacher daily for 30–60 minutes to supplement core instruction.
1, 2, 3	Cooperative learning	Students can work together in pairs, triads, or quads with a set of guidelines for cooperatively completing and sharing assignments.
1, 2, 3	Learning stations/centers	Provide reading activities for students to practice in a learning center (independent) or learning station (with guided instruction).
1, 2, 3	Nonlinguistic representations	Use graphic representations, pictures, mental images, physical or technological models, kinesthetic activities.
1, 2, 3	Compare and contrast familiar items	Compare and contrast items that are familiar along with the introduction of new items.
1, 2, 3	Graphic organizers (e.g., Venn or Comparison Matrix)	Provide guided practice in the use of graphic organizers. Provide models and ample time for demonstration and practice.
1, 2, 3	Model/demonstrate	Model, demonstrate, use body language, facial cues, visuals, hands-on manipulatives, realia, and total physical response.
Additional:		
Additional:		
Additional:		

Sources: Marzano, 2007; Hill and Flynn, 2008.

ENGLISH LANGUAGE LEARNER INTERVENTIONS *(continued)*

Sample Ninth-Grade Reading Intervention Strategies

Sample Tiers	Intervention Strategies	To be Conducted by the General Education Teacher, Volunteers, Retired Teachers
1, 2, 3	Direct instruction (explicit)	Employ a continuum of effective research-based strategies for increasing opportunities for learning by highly qualified teachers in the general education environment.
1, 2, 3	Study buddy/partner	At the beginning of class students are paired with a homogenous or heterogeneous partner that they can study with during class. During this time the students will share and discuss their notes with each other as the teacher monitors their work. (This is not the electronic Study Buddy product.)
1, 2, 3	Cooperative learning	Students work in cooperative homogeneous or heterogeneous pairs, triads, quads with set responsibilities for completing assignments or sharing information.
2, 3	Interactive journal	Students use a composition book to write their feelings, experiences, or responses to prompts. In this case the student kept a journal of his responses to the nonfiction books that he read each week.
2, 3	Nonlinguistic representations	Use graphic representations, pictures, mental images, physical or technological models, kinesthetic activities.
2, 3	Alternative teaching	Students requiring targeted or intensive instruction may be gathered in a small group prior to the class lesson to discuss new vocabulary or preview concepts for 3–4 minutes. The remainder of the class may complete an entrance slip or bell ringer/warm-up activity.
2, 3	Graphic organizers (Cornell Notes and Comparison Matrix)	There are numerous advance organizers (such as Cornell Notes, or double-entry journals) to help students focus and organize information. Once students have learned the method of organizing information, they can make their own organizers as well. A large variety of graphic organizers are available online.
Additional:		
Additional:		
Additional:		

Sources: Marzano, 2007; Hill and Flynn, 2008.

APPENDIX I
Cornell Notes/Double-Entry Journal

Name: _____ Subject/topic: _____

Date: _____

Essential Question:	
Key words:	**Details:**
Summary/Reminders:	

References

Ainsworth, L. (2007). *Common formative assessment.* Thousand Oaks, CA: Corwin Press.

Ainsworth, L., & Christinson, J. (2006). *Five easy steps to a balanced math program for secondary grades: Middle school and high school.* Englewood, CO: Lead + Learn Press.

American Speech-Language-Hearing Association (ASHA). (2003). *23rd annual report to Congress on the implementation of the Individuals with Disabilities Education Act, part B.* Rockville, MD: Author.

Anderson, L. W., & Krathwohl, D. R. (Eds.). (2000). *A taxonomy for learning, teaching, and assessing: A revision of Bloom's taxonomy of educational objectives.* Columbus, OH: Allyn & Bacon.

Applebaum, M. (2009). *The one stop guide to implementing RTI: Academic and behavioral interventions, k–12.* Thousand Oaks, CA: Corwin Press/Sage.

Bender, W. N. (2009). *Beyond the RTI pyramid: Solutions for the first years of implementation.* Bloomington, IN: Solution Tree Press.

Bender, W. N., & Shores, C. (2007). *Response to intervention: A practical guide for every teacher.* Arlington, VA: Council of Exceptional Children.

Bloom, B. S. (1956). *Taxonomy of educational objectives, handbook 1: Cognitive domain.* New York: David McKay.

Brown-Chidsey, R., Bronaugh, L., & McGraw, K. (2009). *RTI in the classroom: Guidelines and recipes for success.* New York: Guilford Press.

Carrell, P. (2007). *Notetaking strategies and their relationship to performance on listening comprehension and communicative assessment tasks.* Princeton, NJ: Educational Testing Service (ETS) and Test of English as a Foreign Language (TOEFL).

Child with a Disability, Rules and Regulations, 34 C.F.R. § 300.8(c)(10)(i)(ii) (2004).

Colorado State Department of Education (CDE). (2008). *Response to intervention (RTI): A practitioner's guide to implementation.* Denver, CO: CDE.

Ehren, B. J., Ehren, T. C., & Proly, J. L. (2009). *Response to intervention: An action guide for school leaders.* Alexandria, VA: Education Research Service (ERS).

Elementary and Secondary Education/No Child Left Behind Act (ESEA/NCLB). (2001). PL 107–110.

Fuchs, D., Fuchs, L. S., & Vaughn, S. (2008). *Response to intervention: A framework for reading educators.* Nashville, TN: National Research Center on Learning Disabilities.

Gardner, H. E. (2004). *Frames of mind: The theory of multiple intelligences.* New York: Basic Books.

Haager, D., Klingner, J., & Vaughn, S. (2007). *Evidence-based reading for response to intervention.* Baltimore, MD: Paul H. Brookes Publishing.

Heacox, D. (2002). *Differentiating instruction in the regular classroom: How to reach and teach all learners, grades 3–12.* St. Paul, MN: Free Spirit Publishing.

Hill, J. D., & Flynn, K. M. (2008). *Classroom instruction that works with English language learners.* Alexandria, VA: ASCD.

House, S. N. (Ed.). (2002). *Behavior intervention manual: Goals, objectives, and intervention strategies.* Columbia, MO: Hawthorne Educational Services.

House, S. N. (Ed.). (2004). *Learning intervention manual: Goals, objectives, and intervention strategies.* Columbia, MO: Hawthorne Educational Services.

Howard, M. (2008). *Response to intervention: Practical strategies for intervening with students before they fall too far behind in reading (grades 1–5).* Bellevue, WA: Bureau of Education and Research.

ldonline.org. *Response to Intervention.* Retrieved on October 1, 2009, from http://www.idonline.org

Individuals with Disabilities Education Improvement Act (IDEIA). Determining the existence of a specific learning disablity. Federal Register, Vol. 71, No. 156, Rules and Regulations, p. 46786, §300.309. Retrieved on March 7, 2012 from http://idea.ed.gov/download/finalregulations.pdf

Institute of Education Sciences. *What Works Clearinghouse.* http://ies.ed.gov/ncee/wwc/

Jimerson, S. R., Burns, M. K., & VanDerHeyden, A. (2007). *Handbook of response to intervention: The science and practice of assessment and intervention.* New York: Springer Publications.

Krashen, S., & Terrell, T. (1983). *The natural approach: Language acquisition in the classroom.* San Francisco: Alemany Press.

Literacy and Information Communication System (LINCS). http://lincs.ed.gov

Marzano, R. J. (2001). *Classroom instruction that works: Research-based strategies for increasing student achievement.* Alexandria, VA: ASCD.

Marzano, R. J. (2007). *The art and science of teaching: A comprehensive framework for effective instruction.* Alexandria, VA: ASCD.

Muschla, G. R. (2004). *Writing teacher's book of lists.* 2nd ed. San Francisco: Jossey-Bass.

National Association of State Directors of Special Education (NASDSE). (2006). *Response to intervention: Policy considerations and implementation.* Alexandria, VA: NASDSE.

National Center for Learning Disabilities (NCLD). (2006). http://www.ncld.org

National Center on Response to Intervention. Home page. Retrieved on October 1, 2009, from www.rti4success.org

National Council of Teachers of Mathematics (NCTM). http://www.nctm.org/

National Library of Vistual Manipulatives. http://nlvm.usu.edu/

National Research Center on the Gifted and Talented (NRC/GT). University of Connecticut. http://www.gifted.uconn.edu/nrcgt.html

National Research Council on Learning Disabilities (NRCLD). (2006, April). *Integrating RTI within the SLD determination process.* National SEA Conference on SLD Determination, Kansas City, MO.

Peery, A. (2010). *Writing to learn.* 2nd ed. Englewood, CO: Lead + Learn Press.

Pierangelo, R. (2003). *The special educator's book of lists.* San Francisco: Jossey-Bass.

Rathvon, N. (2008). *Effective school interventions: Evidence-based strategies for improving student outcomes.* 2nd ed. New York: Guilford Press.

Reeves, D. B. (2008). *Reframing teacher leadership to improve your school.* Alexandria, VA: ASCD.

Renzulli, J. S., & Reis, S. M. (n.d.). The schoolwide enrichment model: Executive summary. http://www.gifted.uconn.edu/sem/semexec.html

Specific Learning Disability/IDEIA (2004). 20 U.S.C. §1401 (30).

Stein, M., Silbert, J., & Carnine, D. W. (1997). *Designing effective mathematics instruction: A direct instruction approach.* 3rd ed. Saddle River, NJ: Prentice Hall.

Stronge, J. H. (2007). *Qualities of effective teachers.* Alexandria, VA: ASCD.

Visual thesaurus. http://www.visualthesaurus.com/

Wright, J. (2007). *RTI toolkit: A practical guide for schools.* National Professional Resources, Inc. Port Chester, NY: Dude Publishing.

Wright, P. W. D., & Wright, P. D. (2007). *Wrightslaw: Special education law.* 2nd ed. Hartfield, VA: Harbor House Law Press.

Index